How to Build Low Cost Motorhomes

2004 Edition

by Louis C. McClure

Edited by Ben Rosander

How to Build
Low Cost
Motorhomes

by Louis C. McClure
Copyright © 1973 by Louis C. McClure

Originally published by
Trail-R-Club of America
ISBN 0-87593-099-9

2004 Edition
edited by Benjamin F. Rosander
in cooperation with the author

Published by:

Ben Rosander
PO Box 327
Marysville, WA 98270-0327

ISBN 0-9724704-6-8

Author's introduction to the 2004 edition

It is with great pleasure that I announce the re-issue of my book, "How to Build Low Cost Motorhomes." I am happy to collaborate with Mr. Ben Rosander, the author of "How to Select and Convert Your Bus on a Shoestring," in a reissue of my book "How to Build Low Cost Motorhomes". With the exception of the Buyer's Guide, the California Administrative Code and other obsolete information, all of the essential information given in the original book is included. Up-to-date resources for these portions are available through other sources.

This book is not intended to be a blueprint for the conversion of a particular make or model of bus. However, it does contain drawings and specifications for many of the interior furnishings, such as convertible dinettes, convertible sofas, kitchen cabinets, bathroom and wardrobe enclosures, stepwells, overhead cabinets, etc. Minor changes in dimensions will be required due to the differences in coach size and design.

Many options are available and may be included in your plan as you desire, although the basics remain the same for any make or model of bus. Your own imagination and pocketbook will determine which of the many of the features and "extras" you will add. You can design and build anything from the simplest weekend getaway to a luxurious palace on wheels by following the procedures outlined in this book.

Ben and I wish you the best of luck, and may you derive great pleasure and satisfaction from designing and converting your bus into your very own Motorhome!

Louis C. McClure

Editor's Introduction to the 2004 edition

Mr. McClure's *How to Build Low Cost Motorhomes* has stood the test of time and is, in my humble opinion, one of the best works of its kind on the subject. While no book can cover every aspect of the conversion of a bus into a motor home, Cal has provided the basic information that one needs to successfully complete this rewarding project.

While I have done moderate editing of the work and replaced many of the old photos, it is largely as it came off the press in 1973. Mr. McClure's easy to read style and common sense approach to the project will be appreciated by the novice and professional alike. In these pages, Cal provides the information you need in easy to understand everyday terms. You will find detailed plans for dinettes, convertible lounges, step wells, wardrobes, and a myriad of other items you will be constructing.

Is a bus conversion for you? Only you can decide. A bus conversion is not for the timid. **To be successful, you MUST be mechanically inclined and handy with all manner of hand and power tools.** Let's face it, some people should never pick up a hammer. **If you cannot successfully repair furniture, your home's electrical and plumbing systems or plan and build a shed, you should consider a commercially built RV.** You must also be patient, able to visualize and plan, and have fairly deep pockets.

Your challenges will include:

- Locating a mechanically sound and suitable bus to convert.
- Storage.
- Conversion costs.
- Title changes from "bus" to "Motorhome," "House car" (or whatever your state calls it). Some states may require an inspection of the conversion to ensure that it meets code. Be sure to find out what your state requires **before** investing time and money.
- Insurance – **Home conversions are considered high risk and insurance is becoming increasingly more difficult to obtain.** You can usually forget anything beyond liability insurance.
- Hundreds (perhaps thousands) of hours needed to complete the project. If both you and your spouse are not fully committed to the project, you can be sure of friction.
- Ensuring that your conversion meets applicable RV building codes. A good definition of misery is "Spending $25,000 on a 10,000 lb. bus conversion that you can't take out of your driveway."

If you feel you can successfully meet these challenges, welcome to the world of bus conversions. If not, you would be best served by a commercial RV.

In any case, best wishes and good luck,

Ben Rosander
rv-busconversions.com
PO Box 327
Marysville, WA 98270-0327
Email: ben@rv-busconversions.com

~ ~ ~ ~ ~ ~ ~ ~ ~ ~

Note: The original photographs in the 1973 edition were lost when the publisher, Trail-R-Club of America, went out of business decades ago. We have replaced most of the photos in this edition with current ones, trying to retain the basic theme of the original text.

Warning-Disclaimer

This book is designed to provide general information only on the subject matter covered. It is sold with the understanding that the publisher, editor and author are not engaged in rendering legal, accounting, engineering, or other professional services. If legal or other expert assistance is required, the services of a competent professional should be sought.

No book of this type can include all available information on every type of bus or every aspect of bus conversions. You are therefore urged to read other available materials and learn as much as possible about bus conversions and to tailor the information to your individual needs.

While every effort has been made to make this book as complete and as accurate as possible, there may be mistakes both typographical and in content. Therefore, this text should be used only as a general guide and not as the ultimate source of bus conversion information.

The purpose of this manual is to educate and entertain. The author, editor and publisher shall have neither liability nor responsibility to any person or entity with respect to any loss or damage caused, or alleged to be caused, directly or indirectly by the information contained in this book.

If you do not wish to be bound by the above, you may return this book to the publisher within five days of purchase for a refund of the purchase price.

Important note to the 2004 edition:

Many references in this book are made to "The Code" and "Appendix".
There are also many "imperatives" in the instructions
using terms such as "shall" "will" and "must".

These references and instructions refer to the
1971 California Administrative Code as it relates to RVs.
As this information is decades out of date it is not included in this edition.
Use these instructions with discretion
and refer to current codes for your state.

If your state does not have an RV building code, refer to
NFPA 1192 Standard on Recreational Vehicles.
This book is available from the National Fire Protection Association
http://www.nfpa.org   Enter "1192" in the search box.

If your conversion does not meet these standards,
you may be unable to register/insure your conversion.

Editor

Table of Contents

Preface

THIS BOOK is intended to help YOU, the average DO-IT-YOURSELFER, to properly design and convert a bus into a COMFORTABLE, LUXURIOUS, COMPLETELY SELF-CONTAINED MOTOR COACH, which you will be proud to own.

There are many makes, models, types, and sizes of used buses that are suitable for conversion into a motor coach. Likewise, there are many suitable floorplan arrangements which may be designed. It would be literally impossible to catalog all the makes and models of buses, along with all the possible floorplan arrangements which may be employed.

There are no two people who have exactly the same likes and dislikes. Likewise, there is no single make, model, size or type of bus, and no single, universal floorplan arrangement, which will fulfill the needs, likes and dislikes of all people. Therefore, this book is designed to show you how to design a floorplan arrangement to accommodate your own family, incorporating your own ideas and arrangements, how to select a suitable bus for conversion, and how to perform the actual conversion of the bus into your very own motor coach.

This book, therefore, is not a blueprint for the conversion of a single make or model of bus into a specific motorcoach arrangement. However, there are a number of drawings, etc., concerning the construction of conventional built-in furnishings, cabinets, etc., which are somewhat universal in nature. In some cases, the drawings may have to be modified slightly to accommodate variations in the bus construction and/or dimensions. However, the basic design of the built-ins remains essentially the same.

Some of the problems faced by the do-it-yourself converter, such as the design and installation of the electrical system, water distribution system, drainage system, and LPG (Liquefied Petroleum Gas) systems are discussed in considerable detail. These discussions are based upon accepted construction codes.

In addition to the technical discussions contained in the book, you will also find other valuable information such as Safety, Maintenance and Operation of your motorcoach. It is suggested that the converter secure a copy of the National Fire Protection Association booklet, NFPA 1192. This guide is available from the National Fire Protection Association, 1 Batterymarch Park, Quincy, Massachusetts 02169-7471. http://www.ngpa.org

There are special chapters concerning appliances and accessories for motor coach installation. There are special sections describing various plumbing fittings and methods of assembly.

The methods presented in this book have been tried and proven. It is the Author's sincere hope that you will find this book to be of great value to you when designing and converting your bus into a motor coach. Compiling this book has truly been a labor of love.

May I take this opportunity to wish you the best of luck, and may you derive great pleasure and self-satisfaction from designing and converting your bus into your very own motor coach!

Louis C. McClure, Sr., Author

1. How to Build Low Cost Motorhomes

Did you ever wish you could afford a motor coach? Well, believe it or not, you can now own one for less than the retail price of a new pickup truck with cab-over camper or modern travel trailer!

If you are a do-it-yourselfer, have ordinary hand tools, average skill, and adequate time, there's no good reason why you cannot convert a used bus into a modern, custom-designed motor coach. So why settle for anything less?

Most people who have ever owned a motor coach will tell you that it is the only way to go. Many of them have progressed from a tent, to a truck-mounted camper or travel trailer, to a motor coach.

Just how much does it cost to convert a bus into a motor coach, anyway? Well, there's no fixed cost; it varies over very wide ranges from just a few hundred dollars for the simplest units, up to you-name-it for the deluxe custom-converted palaces on wheels.

Of course, there's one catch: you've got to do the work of designing and converting the bus yourself! However, if you follow the easy, step-by-step instructions I have laid down for you in this book — you can have a beautiful, converted unit that you can be justifiably proud of — one that you have designed and converted to fit your family's exact needs and desires. It will be uniquely yours — designed and constructed to accommodate you and your family in luxury and comfort.

Many people have dreamed of having their own motor coach and some have bought a used bus to convert. However, some became concerned they did not have sufficient knowledge or ability to carry the project through to its completion. If you happen to be one of these people — cheer up! This book was written just for you!

A used bus is a logical vehicle to convert into a motor coach. They are usually larger than other types of self-propelled van-type vehicles, and provide sufficient inside space to permit building a comfortable, luxurious unit.

An important advantage of converting a used bus into a motor coach is that the entire chassis and body are already constructed. All we have to do is to design and build the interior according to your own plans. That is easy to say — and that is precisely what this book is all about.

Buses are built by manufacturers who have had long years of experience in their design and construction. They are properly engineered for the purpose for which they were intended. The chassis was designed to accommodate the full rated payload with ample safety factor and they are among the safest vehicles on the road. Buses were designed to last many times longer than an automobile. Many twenty-year-old buses are still in regular public service!

Buses are available in lengths from perhaps twenty feet for the smallest school buses, to forty-five feet for the interstate and transit types. Most buses are a standard eight feet wide overall.

There are several basic types of buses available. These are (1) the conventional, engine-and-hood-out-front type; (2) the blunt-nose, engine-up-front type; (3) the blunt-nose, engine-in-rear type, and (4) the blunt-nose, engine amidships, under the floor. I shall discuss some of the advantages and disadvantages of each, but shall not attempt to suggest which type would be best for you. In fact, I have owned two different types, and liked both! See Chapter 2 for a discussion on types of buses available.

There are several very important considerations to be taken into account when designing your motor coach. After due consideration of these, we may make a more intelligent selection of a bus to convert.

The first, and one of the most important considerations, is to determine the number of persons that will normally be using the motor coach at the same time. We must, of course, provide sleeping, dining, cooking, bathroom and storage facilities for the total number of people. A small motor coach may be adequate for only two persons, but can be very crowded for a family of four to six.

Second, how do you plan to use your motor coach? Just for frequent weekend jaunts, and a two-week vacation each year? Or do you plan extended trips in your motor coach — perhaps for a month or more at a time? Or do you plan to live in your coach either part-time or full-time? Generally, the more time you spend in your motor coach, the more you will appreciate the additional space, which a larger unit provides. A small motor coach can seem to "close in" on you during long periods, especially if inclement weather, etc. keeps you indoors much of the time.

Most of the people I have known who have designed and converted a bus into a motor coach take their unit out on a "trial run" before it is completed. I would strongly recommend doing so. This way you can get the real feel for how you want it arranged while you still have the opportunity to make the changes. Also, you can determine how comfortable and livable your motor coach is or will be. Remember that your motor coach is your very own production, your own ideas and plans transformed into reality. The ultimate test is your own satisfaction and enjoyment.

Now let us return to the problem of designing a motor coach. Be sure to give careful consideration to the preliminary determinations mentioned earlier: how many persons will be using the coach at one time, how you plan to use the coach; and the degree of self-containment required. After we have determined these basic requirements, we are ready to proceed with the design of our own "dream-home-on-wheels".

No two people have exactly the same likes and dislikes. Similarly, there is no single motor coach floor plan that will completely satisfy everyone. Consequently, motor coaches are designed with many different floor plans. No one can say which is best for anyone else. The choice of a floor plan is a highly individual, personal matter. Your own personality, likes and dislikes are reflected in your

Here and on the following pages we have included a number of photographs and drawings from both home and professionally converted coaches, illustrating many of the available options. Study them carefully and incorporate those features that interest you into your own design.

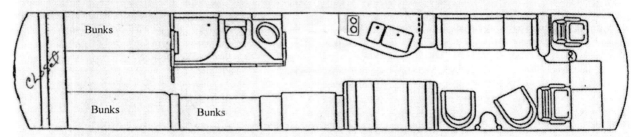

Three sets of bunk beds. Bunks can be either two or three high as room and needs dictate. With "pusher" engines, the area aft of the bed is a natural place for a closet. Most dinettes are convertible, providing additional bed space.

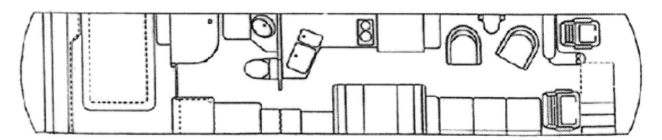

Side master bed design with center aisle. Space requirements in the master bedroom are often underestimated and care should be taken to ensure there is enough room to walk around the bed easily. In many coaches, getting in and out and making the bed requires squeeze play. Side bed designs often work best with a side aisle (shown on next page).

Floor plans courtesy of Walker Private Coach

motor coach.

So, where do we start? The following will highlight some of the considerations involved. Using this example as your starting point, plug in your situation, preferences and tastes. Then factor in your budget and make modifications as best suits you.

Statistics tell us that there are 3.9 persons in the average family, so let's create a hypothetical family of four consisting of two parents and two adolescent/teenage children, a boy and girl.

The parent's employment provides for a two-week vacation each year. They live in a city, and like to get out into the boon-docks on weekends. On their vacation, they may take a cross-country trip in their coach.

Our hypothetical family lives in a city, but has a yard large enough and accessible to permit them to legally park the bus at home. The husband has average do-it-yourself skills, and owns or has access to the needed tools and equipment.

Now that we have a profile of our "hypothetical family", let's take a look at some options and considerations.

First, we must provide sleeping, dining, cooking, bathroom and storage facilities for four. Additionally, consider the possibility that you or your children may be inviting guests and plan accordingly. It is far better to have an extra unused bed than to be short.

While the parents may prefer a full-size bed, a convertible sofa, gaucho-bed, or twin beds, let's suppose they prefer a full size bed.

The children, a boy and a girl, should have separate sleeping accommodations. They may have a convertible dinette and a sofa, bunk beds, or a dinette and an overhead bunk. For our discussion, let's suppose they prefer bunk beds. (Most children do). Later, when the children are away from home, at college, in service, married, etc., the bunk beds may be removed if desired and other use made of

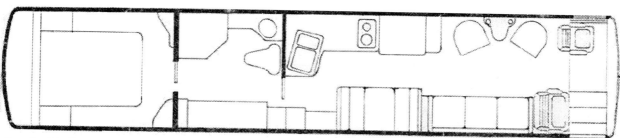

Standard in-line master bed design with center aisle. Note use of pocket doors. Standard hinged doors often get in the way in close quarters.

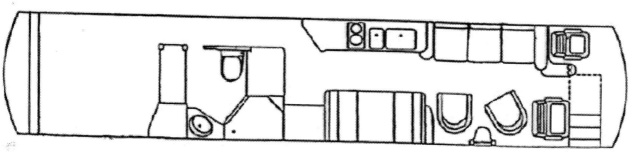

Side aisle design. This plan enables the bathroom to be roomier and opens up layout options. The master bed can easily be set for either side or in-line configuration.

Floor plans courtesy of Walker Private Coach

the available space.

Dining facilities should be provided to seat four persons comfortably. This may be in the form of a standard-type dinette, a U-shaped dinette, or twin divans with the table mounted between. In each case, the table should be removable to provide additional sleeping accommodations if needed. The dining facilities may be included as a regular part of the sleeping accommodations using the convertible dinette discussed in Chapter 7.

The kitchen usually consists of a range and oven, base cabinet with single or twin sinks, a refrigerator or ice box, and storage space for utensils, food, dishes, silverware, etc. A four or six cubic foot refrigerator is recommended as a minimum - larger if you have a larger family

The bathroom usually consists of a toilet, shower, lavatory, and medicine cabinet. Probably the only difference in the bathroom facilities for larger families would be in water and holding tank capacities.

In general, it is advisable to provide as much water, holding tank, and propane gas (LPG) capacity as practical in any motor coach.

Other types of storage, such as wardrobes, chests of drawers, cabinets, etc., must also be provided. It is suggested that at least one running foot of ceiling-to-floor wardrobe space be provided for each adult or adolescent. There should also be at least one good-sized drawer for each person to store personal articles, clothing, etc. Small children may require more drawer and cabinet space, and less wardrobe space. Cove cabinets should be installed wherever possible, but should not interfere with headroom or freedom of movement.

Knowing the family's requirements and preferences, we can now proceed to design a floor plan which fits their needs. (This is the same procedure you would use to design your own motor coach floor plan to fit your family's needs. Merely make the necessary changes or substitutions in the example, and follow the same procedure).

To facilitate making your floor plan, we have provided a handy grid, representing the floor of the proposed motor coach on Page 10. Each square in the grid represents one square foot. As we mentioned earlier, most buses suitable for conversion are eight feet wide outside, and approximately seven and one-half feet wide inside. The heavy longitudinal lines on each side of the grid represent the sidewalls of the bus, and are so spaced

"Michaela"

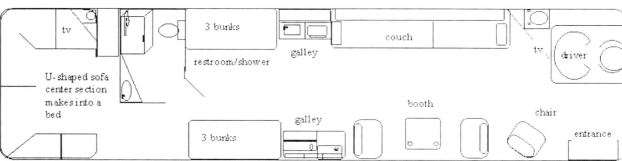

to represent seven and one-half feet net interior width.

The grid, therefore, represents a floor that is seven and one-half feet wide (inside) by forty feet long. When you acquire your bus, take careful measurements and adjust the grid to suit your bus.

We have also provided templates representing various commonly used built-in items, such as beds, divans, dinettes, wardrobes, bathrooms, etc. These templates are drawn to the same scale as the grid, i.e.; one square equals one square foot. Typical dimensions of the standard built-ins are also given.

Feel free to photocopy and enlarge the template found on Page 10 of this book. Alternatively, you may obtain a large piece of graph paper and make your own larger scale templates and scale features using construction paper. Large sheets of graph paper are sold in most office supply stores as desk blotters. Then, using a pair of scissors or a penknife, cut out the templates. Leave the bold lines on the template. Now it will be found that the overall dimensions of the template agree with the dimensions shown on the template as well as on the grid.

It has been my experience that it is easier to begin at some known starting point such as the rear end wall, partition, etc., and work forward. Place the templates on the grid in any desired arrangement and shuffle them around as you please.

One of the most popular configurations places the master bedroom at the rear of the coach, followed by the bathroom on one side of the coach with a closet on the other. The bunk beds are then placed next, followed by the kitchen and living area. This allows for privacy in the master bedroom and ensured that no one will have to pass through someone else's sleeping quarters for late night trips to the bathroom. Additionally, the door to the master bedroom and another at the entry to the closet/bathroom area can work together to create a large change area. (The top floor plan on Page 3 illustrates the cooperating door principle.)

"Michaela" is a 40-foot 1988 MCI luxuriously converted in 2004 It sleeps eight with a seating capacity of 12.

The bus has 6 bunks and rear lounge that makes into queen bed. The rear lounge has a walk in closet and a complete entertainment center.

This unit also features a 10 KW Onan diesel generator, three Coleman roof air conditioners, a built in TV antenna, and a full bath with 32" walk in shower. A second complete entertainment center is located in the front lounge.

"Michaela" courtesy of Wayne Harper

Some conversions place the bunk area in the front of the bus, but since the main entry door is also located in front, this can prove to be an inconvenience and affords little privacy.

It is usually desirable to have the dining area adjacent to or across the aisle from the kitchen for convenience in dining. This necessitates the kitchen and dinette being located toward the front of the coach. We must also provide for the location of the bathroom. Ideally, the bathroom should be located between the sleeping areas so it is not necessary to pass through someone else's sleeping area to reach it.

Any bathroom arrangement may be used. Those shown in the templates and floor plans are intended to be representative only.

The only remaining provision we must make is for the location of wardrobes. We may find that we have sufficient space available opposite the bathroom. This would be an ideal location, as the doors of the bathroom and wardrobe may be designed to cooperate with each other when opened, and provide a convenient dressing area.

With our basic design in mind, we may then proceed to refine our floor plan, and to analyze it to determine that it fully meets our requirements. We may make modifications of the floor plan as we desire. When we have arrived at the desired floor plan arrangement, we merely count the number of squares from front to rear. This will determine the MINIMUM amount of clear, unobstructed (except for wheel wells) floor space we must have between the rear end wall or partition and the rear of the driver's seat to accommodate our needs.

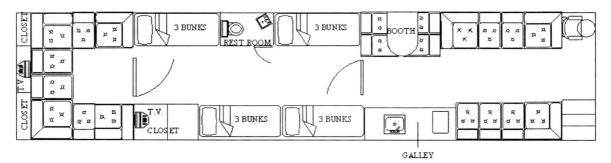

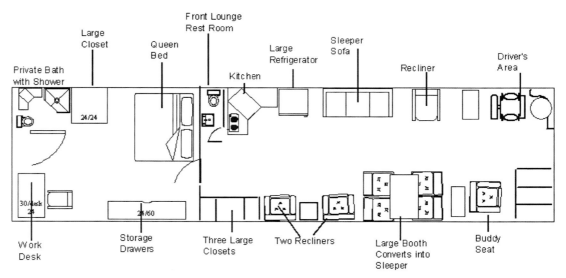

Top: 1993 Prevost LeMirage Entertainer bus

Bottom: 1999 MCI Renaissance

Floor plans courtesy of Staley Coach

There are a number of tried-and-proven floor plans included with this chapter. You may wish to use one of these floor plans, or possibly you may use a combination of two or more to arrive at the design that best meets your needs. There are an endless number of possible arrangements.

Kitchens should be designed to be as convenient as possible. This means that the range, oven, sink, and refrigerator should be conveniently arranged with respect to each other, to save steps and prevent unnecessary congestion. Aisles in motor coaches are necessarily narrow, and the kitchen is usually more congested than any other area.

All kitchen appliances may be located on the same side of the bus if desired. This arrangement often simplifies the installation of the plumbing, electrical, and gas lines later.

Provide as much counter-top workspace and storage space in the kitchen as possible. This is more important if the motor coach is to be used for extended travel or living. Thus, you can stock sufficient food and supplies to last for several days or weeks.

There are several types of ranges and range-ovens available for installation in motor coaches. The simplest is the small two-or-three burner "hot plate". This unit requires a minimum amount of space, and permits the installation of a variety of refrigerators or iceboxes below the cook top. Or, additional storage space may be provided under the range. Another type is the three or four burner range with oven, which are made in special "short" models, only 16 inches high overall. These also

provide storage space beneath the oven. Other three and four burner range/ovens are available, only 20 inches high. These are essentially the same as the "short" models, except the oven is larger. So-called "apartment-size" ranges with oven and broiler are often used. These units are 36" high, 20" to 22" wide, and twenty-four inches deep. They are freestanding, and do not require being built-in. They match standard base cabinets in height and depth.

Three or four burner ranges with separate overhead ovens above are available, and are quite popular in motor coaches. However, they may present an installation problem in some converted buses, due to the interference between the upper rear edge of the oven and the low radius ceiling of the bus. Most factory-made motor homes which use this type of range and oven have straight-sided walls instead of the radius walls common in buses.

Refrigerators or iceboxes may be obtained which are designed to fit either in the kitchen base cabinets, or to be installed in an elevated position in a wall cabinet. Generally, a four cubic foot gas/electric refrigerator or a seventy-five pound capacity icebox can be installed in the kitchen base cabinet under the counter. Larger units are available, but must be installed either freestanding or in a wall cabinet. When the smaller, under-the-counter types are used, additional kitchen workspace is available. Many factory-made motor homes suffer from a lack of sufficient counter top workspace in the kitchen.

Base cabinets may either be custom-made, standard, unfinished, ready-made cabinets, or steel base cabinets as desired. Custom-made cabinets may be

Floor plan for a 1984 GMC school bus

"I ended up veering from this original plan, and this was a recommendation from one of the books I read. As with many building projects, it is good to start with a well-thought plan, but remain flexible enough to make necessary changes. " Chris Jeub.

made the exact length required, and to accommodate any given size of range, refrigerator, sink, etc. If a freestanding apartment-size range is installed, standard 42, 54, or 66-inch long steel base cabinets may be installed if desired.

As was mentioned earlier, storage space should be provided wherever possible. All areas such as under beds, sofas, dinettes, and kitchen cabinets should be converted into storage space. Also, cove cabinets, should be installed at the junction of the sidewall and roof, wherever they do not interfere with other built-ins, doorways, appliances, or create hazards. Additional storage space beneath or on top of the motor coach may also be provided.

There are endless combinations which may be used when designing your motor coach floor plan. The ideas and floor plans presented here are by no means the only ones that may be used. However, they are all tried and proven, and careful consideration should be given to them. If you have a better method of designing your motor coach than that presented here, by all means use it. However, you will not go wrong by using the ideas and

suggestions presented in this book. After the desired floor plan has been determined, it is suggested that you prepare accurate scale-size drawings of the floor plan arrangement, showing the plan view and the right and left sidewall elevation in register. This drawing will be of great help later, when planning the plumbing, electrical, and gas systems in your motor coach.

It is highly recommended that anyone planning a motor coach floor plan get all the information available before proceeding. Visit motor home sales lots, attend recreational vehicle shows, read all available magazines relating to motor homes, talk with motor home and motor coach owners, etc. You will find them very enthusiastic about their coaches, and anxious to give you any advice, suggestions, etc., which you may desire. Remember that their motor coaches are very close to their hearts.

Take plenty of time to plan your motor coach floor plan. Do not rush. You may have to live with it for a long time. Get all the information you can, then proceed. Good Luck!

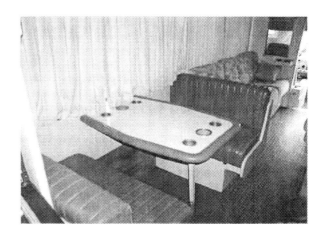

This beautiful 1987 MCI Executive Coach was built by Custom Coach. It features a separate driver's cabin complete with its own sound system and co-pilot's seat. The coach seats 22 and sleeps five.

Deluxe appointments include Corinthian leather sofas, Corian countertops and central vacuum.

Courtesy of Colonial Coach Lines

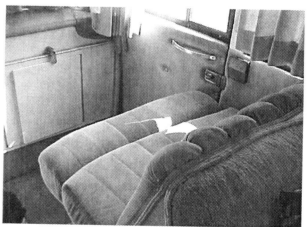

This classic 1955 GMC Scenicruiser was beautifully converted to a deluxe motor coach in 1996. The dinette converts into a bed, as does the lower level lounge couch. The lounge serves as the entry way and a sitting area providing a nice place to entertain separate from the living quarters . The couches are lounging couches and can be used in both sitting and reclined positions.

While the Scenicruiser is one of the classics of the bus industry, it creates unique challenges for converters because of the multi-leveled floor.

Photos courtesy of Larry McGuire

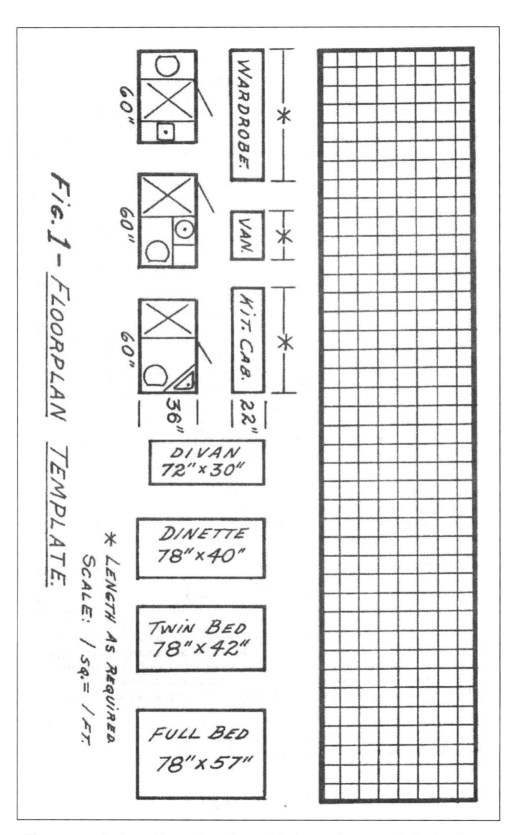

Fig. 1 - FLOORPLAN TEMPLATE.

WARDROBE. 60"

VAN. 60"

KIT. CAB. 22" 60" 36"

DIVAN 72" x 30"

DINETTE 78" x 40"

TWIN BED 78" x 42"

FULL BED 78" x 57"

* LENGTH AS REQUIRED
SCALE: 1 SQ. = 1 FT.

Photocopy and enlarge this template, if you wish, then cut it out to assist in planning your motor coach.

Note: See the Table of Abbreviations on page 122 for the key to floor plans.

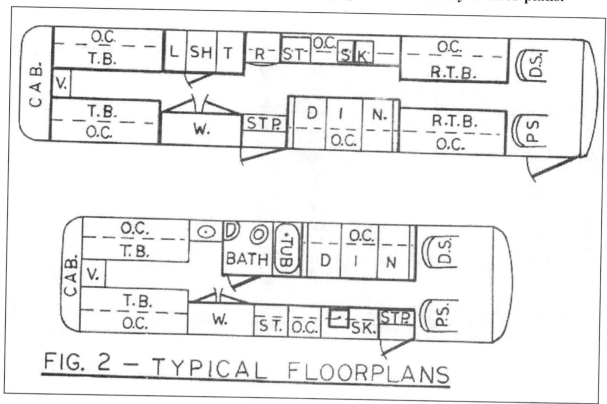

FIG. 2 — TYPICAL FLOORPLANS

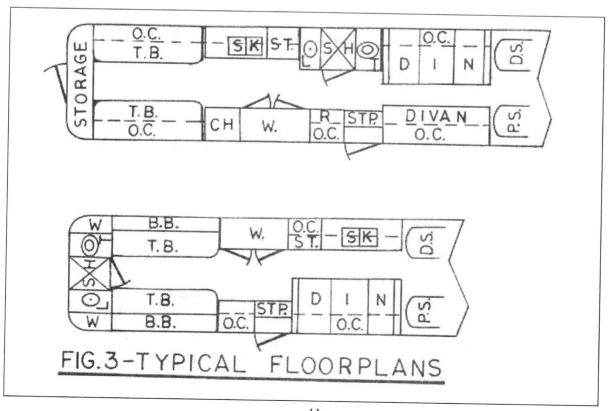

FIG. 3 — TYPICAL FLOORPLANS

11

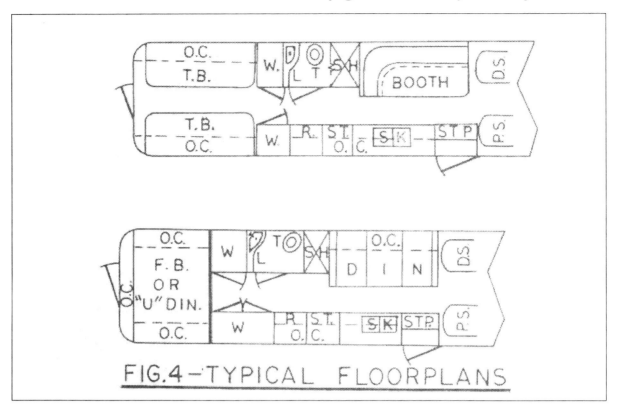

FIG.4 – TYPICAL FLOORPLANS

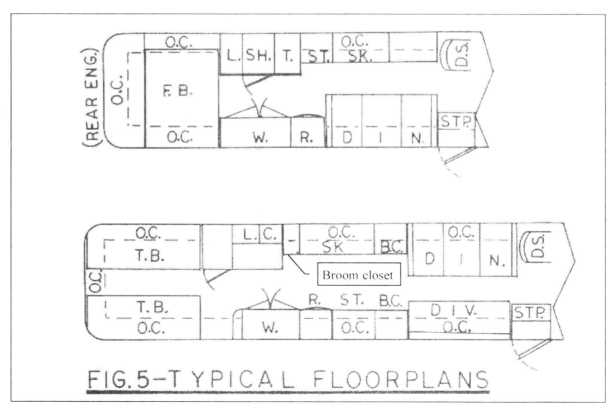

FIG.5 – TYPICAL FLOORPLANS

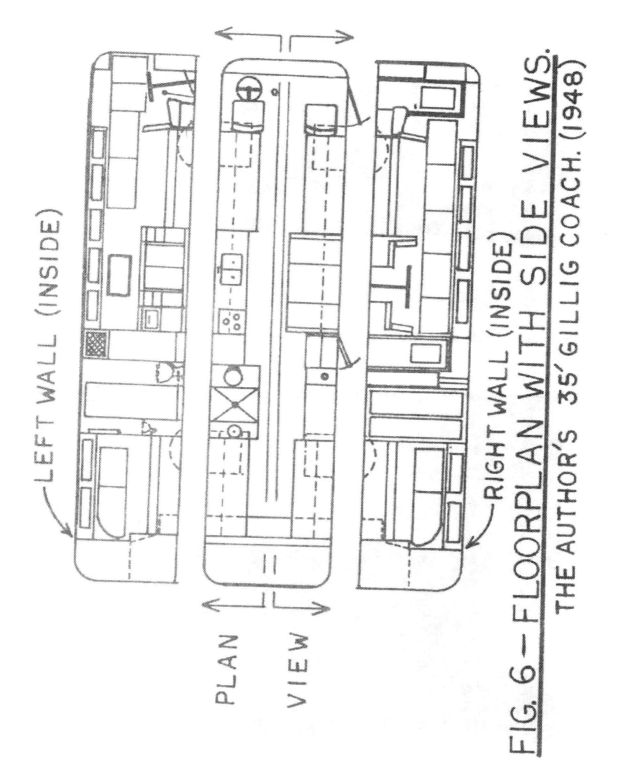

LEFT WALL (INSIDE)

PLAN VIEW

RIGHT WALL (INSIDE)

FIG. 6 — FLOORPLAN WITH SIDE VIEWS.
THE AUTHOR'S 35' GILLIG COACH. (1948)

Photos of this bus conversion are on the next page.

Above and below: The author's 1948 Gillig is a 35-foot diesel pusher.

Below (Looking forward): The **reclining twin beds**, immediately behind the driver, double as lounges chairs. Hinged in the center, each end can fold up, facing forward while on the road, or aft when parked. A table is placed between them for dining, and can comfortably seat six adults. Plans for these reclining twin beds start on Page 40.

The driver and co-pilots seats are from an old Corvair. Note the convenient folding table (barely seen folded down) in front of the co-pilot.

2. Types of Buses

There are four basic types of buses, the conventional, engine and hood-out-front type, often referred to as a conventional, or school bus type, and the blunt-nosed type. The blunt-nosed type is available in a blunt-nose, front-engine type, blunt-nose, rear-engine type, and a blunt-nose, amidships-engine type. The amidships-engine type has the engine mounted between the front and rear axles, approximately midway of the bus, under the floor. All types are available with either gasoline or diesel engines.

CONVENTIONAL BUSES:

Conventional buses, often referred to as "school buses", are typified by the smaller, older school buses. Usually, the chassis is made by one of the popular truck manufacturers, and the body is made by one of several manufacturers specializing in bus bodies. These body manufacturers design their bodies to fit the popular bus chassis made by the major truck manufacturers. So, if some of the names appear unfamiliar to you, you will probably recognize the chassis manufacturer immediately.

Many people dislike the conventional-type bus because it reminds them of a school bus. Somehow they do not have as much public appeal for use as a motor coach as do the blunt-nosed units. This may well be, but the conventional bus has some strong advantages to recommend it.

As we mentioned earlier, they are usually constructed on one of the more popular truck manufacturer's chassis, such as Ford, Chevrolet, Dodge, GMC, International, etc. Therefore, parts are easily obtained. Almost any crossroads town will have a dealer, or least on automotive parts store where most chassis parts can be readily obtained.

Secondly, conventional buses are usually lighter than the blunt-nosed types. Conventional buses are made in overall

lengths from about twenty to thirty-five feet. They are the most common types of elementary school buses, and are usually more readily available than the blunt-nosed types. Often they are also priced lower than the blunt-nosed type bus.

In addition to having the engine and hood out front, which classifies them as school-bus types, they may have low ceilings. Ceiling heights of only five feet eight inches to five feet ten inches are common in older models. This is because they were primarily designed for transporting school children rather than adults, and the higher ceilings were not required. Later models have increased ceiling heights, however, of approximately six feet. Be sure to determine whether you can stand up comfortably in any bus, which you would consider for conversion. Most of the conventional military buses have ceilings of six feet or more.

School buses may have gross vehicle weights from 12,000 to 26,000 pounds. They are conservatively designed to safely carry the maximum number of persons that they will seat. Ample safety margins are built in. School buses are also designed for maximum safety. They have all-metal bodies, bolted, welded, or riveted to all metal frames. School buses are among the safest vehicles on the road.

Here is a 1988 International school bus converted into a recreational vehicle. This type of unit is among the most economical to convert and the most readily available. One can make these conversions as simple or elaborate as desired, based on needs and budgets. These units offer fun with economy.

Photo courtesy of Rick and Myrna Russell

"BruinGilda the AeroSwine"

Here is an example of a 1976 International/Wayne school bus converted into a deluxe motor coach.

School buses, affectionately known as "sKOOLies", have one distinct advantage over highway coaches: high ground clearance. In addition to ease of maintenance and greater parts availability, sKOOLies are not strictly limited to flat terrain, RV parks and rest areas. SKOOLies are often seen on logging roads and at fishing holes where a highway coach would high center before getting 20 feet off the pavement. Just make sure to scout ahead in unknown backwoods areas before venturing down the path with your bus. Unwelcome surprises can result in a hefty towing bill or having to back out on a narrow, winding path with no place to turn around.

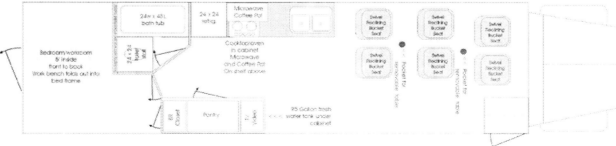

Photos and floor plan courtesy of Joe Petty

16

School buses are usually designed for relatively short, stop-and-go driving. Most states limit the speed of school buses to 50 miles per hour. Therefore, school buses are designed to operate in this speed range. They may be repowered, (a more powerful engine installed) and a lower numerical ratio rear axle gear installed, permitting them to be operated at higher speeds, but this is an expensive operation.

Some conventional buses are designed for adult use. In this case, the ceiling has been raised, either by the addition of fixed windows and spacers above the standard windows, or using taller windows on the sides.

Conventional buses can be converted into excellent motor coaches, and at a reasonable cost. They can provide many years of happy, trouble-free service so, unless you have a hang-up about conventional-type buses, this may be well worth your serious consideration.

TRANSIT-TYPE BUSES:

The blunt-nosed, transit type bus is very popular for conversion into a motor coach. There are three basic arrangements of the transit bus, (blunt-nosed, front engine; blunt-nosed, rear engine; and blunt-nosed, amidships engine), all of which are used for conversion.

The blunt-nosed bus is considered more desirable for conversion into a motor coach. They may be equipped with either gasoline or diesel engines.

Transit-type buses are generally designed for relatively short run, lower speed, stop-and-go driving, such as for intracity bus lines. Many transit-type buses are also used for school buses.

Most transit-type bus drive components are made by one of the large truck manufacturers, while the chassis and body are made by one of the specialized bus body manufacturers. Many brand names on transit coaches may be unfamiliar, but the drive train manufacturer would be recognized immediately.

Transit buses are generally heavier than the conventional buses. They are available in lengths from approximately 25 to 40 feet.

Transit buses provide a maximum of interior usable space for conversion into a motor coach. The engine may be installed within the coach, as in the case of a front or rear engine model, and greater use may be made of the overall length. In the case of the conventional bus, the length represented by the engine and hood are essentially lost so far as conversion is concerned.

In the blunt-nosed, front engine type of transit bus, the driver's seat is located beside the engine, therefore occupying essentially the same area inside the coach as the engine. The door is usually located opposite the driver, making maximum use of this space. However, the location of the engine hood immediately in front of the door makes for more inconvenient entrance and exit from the coach. In this case, it is usually desirable to relocate the main entrance door elsewhere.

Front-engine transit types are often- noisier than other types. This is because the driver and possibly a passenger are sitting immediately adjacent to the engine. In some models, conversation is difficult due to normal engine noises. Also, heat radiation into the coach in warm weather can be a problem.

It is usually necessary to service the engine from within the coach. There is always the danger of spilling oil, water, grease, fuel, etc., on the floor or carpet while servicing the unit.

Due to the fact that the engine is located in the front of the coach, the entire floor area from the rear of the driver's seat to the rear wall is available for conversion. Therefore, a given floor plan can often be installed in a transit bus, which is shorter overall than would be required to install the same floor plan in a conventional bus.

The rear-engine transit bus is also very popular for conversion into a motor coach. In this case, as in the case of the front-engine models, the drive train is usually made by one of the major truck manufacturers, while a specialized bus body manufacturer makes the chassis and body.

The rear-engine transit type does not provide quite as much free inside space as does the front-engine transit type, due to the space occupied by the engine. This may be approximately three feet in the rear of the coach in a representative model.

However, the rear engine transit type is usually easier to service, as access doors or panels open on all sides of the engine. The noise generated by the engine inside the coach is considerably reduced, as the engine is located as much as 30 feet behind the driver's compartment.

Rear-engine transit types are more prone to overheating than are the conventional or front-engine transit types buses. This is probably because of starvation for air due to the airflow along the sides of the bus, especially when the wind is coming from the side opposite the radiator. The cooling system must receive constant attention to prevent the danger of overheating.

The amidships-engine type of transit bus offers the most available inside space for its length of any type. In this case, the engine is usually a flat, "pancake" type, mounted under the floor of the bus. Access to the engine is usually from the outside, although some older models required removing inside floor panels to service the engine. In these cases, it is necessary to arrange the floor plan to permit easy removal and reinstallation of the floor panels.

Some of the amidships pancake engines are no longer being manufactured and parts are difficult to obtain. As with any bus, always determine whether repair and replacement parts are readily available, and at affordable prices, before purchasing the bus. Also, determine whether service can be performed by using ordinary tools, equipment, and skills, or whether specialized tools, fixtures, and equipment are required.

INTERCITY, INTERSTATE BUSES:

The blunt-nosed, intercity or interstate buses, which are ordinarily used for long distance, high-speed operation, are perhaps the most desirable type of bus for conversion into a motor coach. However, they are usually much more expensive to purchase and maintain than either the conventional or the transit type bus.

The intercity bus has all the advantages of the rear-engine or amidships-engine transit type, plus higher cruising speed. In addition, these units are usually more modern than the other types of buses. Surprisingly, the operating costs of intercity or interstate buses are sometimes less than that for the transit type bus!

The intercity or interstate type bus is designed to operate at sustained highway speeds. They also feature better suspension, offer better riding characteristics, and are generally more desirable than other types of buses for conversion. If you can afford the best, this is probably your logical choice.

Custom Eagle coach conversion.
Courtesy of Walker Private Coach

3. Selecting and Buying Buses for Conversion

Now that we have arrived at our desired floor plan arrangement, and therefore know how much space will be required to accommodate our desired floor plan, we are ready to turn to the problem of selecting a suitable bus to convert. Where does a person look for used buses for sale?

The first, and most obvious, would be used bus dealers in your area, which may be listed in the Yellow Pages of your local telephone book. They will be listed under such headings as Buses, Used; Buses, Charter and Rental; or Buses, Distributors and Manufacturers.

The internet has scores of businesses selling buses, both new and used.

Other sources of used buses are the local elementary and high schools; surplus military sales lots; classified sections of the local newspapers; and the Motor Coach Mart, published by the Family Motor Coach Association, P.O. Box 44144, Cincinnati, Ohio. There is no regularly established retail price for used buses. Usually, they sell for whatever the market will bear. Used school buses can sometimes be had for just a few hundred dollars, while deluxe cross-country units may sell for ten thousand dollars or more.

Previously, we determined the amount of interior space that would be required to accommodate our floor plan. But length should not be the only consideration.

The exterior appearance of the bus is of great importance. We are not as concerned with the paint job and other cosmetics as we are the basic lines of the bus and how solid the body is. In areas near salt water, or where salt is used on the streets and roads during winter, expect considerable rust damage. Aluminum bodies are not apt to be as badly affected by corrosion as steel bodies are.

Although rusted areas may be repaired or replaced, it often involves considerable work and expense. Body dents may be repaired provided the metal is not torn or otherwise badly damaged. Sections of metal may be removed and replaced if necessary. This work is both time consuming and expensive.

In many cases, a bus in good condition that has a shabby paint job can be bought very reasonably. You'll be repainting it anyway, so you could hardly care less!

Tires for a bus can be expensive. However, it is perfectly satisfactory to use "recaps" on the dual rear wheels; Make sure the casings are sound, and not badly weather-checked. Tires may be painted with a liquid neoprene compound, which will effectively seal the cracks and make the tire look new again. Also, the cracks will be effectively sealed against further intrusion of moisture and further damage.

Front tires on a bus or motor home should always be first-run rubber, not re-treads or recaps. Make sure the front tires have at least one-sixteenth to one-eighth inch of tread depth at the center of the tread. Inspect all tires for cuts, breaks, bulges, or other signs of damage. Remember that the front tires are critical to your safety. Don't take any unnecessary chances!

Most buses have a manual four- or five-speed transmission. Often the five speed transmissions are overdrive in fifth gear. These transmissions often have a .8:1 ratio in fifth, and 1:1 ratio in fourth

Coaches ready for conversion
Courtesy of Staley Coach

gears. The effect of an overdrive transmission is to give a higher gear for higher road speed and better economy of operation while cruising. The bus will have less pulling power in overdrive than in direct, and it will be necessary to shift back into direct or lower gears in mountainous terrain or when climbing grades.

Two-speed automatic transmissions are found on some of the transit-type buses. These are satisfactory for transit use, but are at best a compromise for motor coach applications and are not recommended for motor coaches. Newer buses are sometimes available with six speed automatic transmissions. These are ideal for motorcoach use, but are usually quite expensive. Two speed rear axles are also found on some buses, particularly used military buses. A two-speed rear axle allows you to select two different rear axle ratios, which effectively doubles the number of transmission/rear axle ratios available. Thus, a bus equipped with a five-speed manual transmission, and a two-speed rear axle, will have a total of ten forward speeds. A two-speed rear axle is very desirable in a motorcoach. The lower speed may be used to gain additional pulling power on grades when needed, and the higher speed ratio may be used for higher speed, more economical cruising.

Power steering is also very desirable for motor coaches, especially if the fairer sex will be driving the coach. Some of the larger buses, which do not have power steering, require considerable strength to maneuver in close quarters.

Be sure to take a test drive in any used bus that you are considering before buying it. Make sure that it steers true, does not have excessive slop in the steering wheel (although this may be just a matter of adjustment), or does not develop front wheel shimmy at certain speeds. (This may be due to wheel balance, kingpin and bushings, steering linkage, wheel bearings, etc.) Insist on these faults being corrected before buying the bus, if possible.

Buses are usually heavy, cumbersome, slow to accelerate, and require much greater turning radii and stopping distances. Engines used in buses are usually designed to deliver maximum torque at a relatively low RPM, in the driving range. The horsepower is somewhat modest. The horsepower-to-weight ratio is very low in comparison to automobile ratios.

Most buses will have either power-assisted (vacuum-boost) hydraulic brakes, or air brakes. In case of air brakes, check the security of the brake system by allowing the pressure indicator to build up to one hundred to one hundred twenty pounds (determined by the governor or regular setting on the air brake system), then apply the brakes full force for one minute. The pressure, as indicated on the pressure gauge, should not leak down more than two pounds from the initial drop when the brakes were applied. If the pressure drops more than two pounds in the first minute, it is an indication of loss of air pressure somewhere in the system. This could well be leakage in a valve, fitting, etc. It may often be isolated by using soapy water, applied to all the fittings in the system.

Many states require all air brake equipped school buses to have "spring brakes" installed with their air brake systems. One popular type of spring brake

In larger communities one can sometimes locate companies that specialize in the sale or conversion of used buses. Prices vary considerably depending on age, type and condition.

Courtesy of Walker Private Coach

system is essentially a pair of heavy coil springs inside special rear wheel actuators, which apply the brakes when the air pressure drops to sixty pounds or less. Also, the spring brakes are applied while the air pressure is building up to sixty pounds. In case of failure of an airline, tank, valve, etc., allowing the pressure to drop to sixty pounds or less, the spring brakes are automatically applied. In normal operation, after the air pressure reaches sixty pounds, the spring brakes are released, and the system operates just as any normal air brake system. At approximately sixty pounds of pressure, a supplemental diaphragm releases the spring brakes by compressing the springs. The system is fully automatic when operating normally.

Should your air pressure leak down or suddenly drop to below sixty pounds, your brakes are automatically applied by the springs.

This is to bring the vehicle to a stop, and prevent runaway in case of air pressure system failure. Simultaneously with a drop of air pressure below sixty pounds, a warning light and buzzer are activated.

In case of failure of the air brake system, and the application of the spring brakes, provisions are made to enable removing the bus from the highway to a garage for repair. An emergency compressed air tank is installed, which receives its pressure from the normal air brake pressure system. A check valve is installed in the inlet to the emergency pressure tank, allowing the air to enter the tank, but preventing it from escaping through the normal air pressure system. The emergency tank is fitted with hand-controlled valves, which permit releasing the spring brakes manually. Pull the valve up to release, and push down to reapply the spring brakes.

Removing the pressure to the hold-off diaphragm permits the spring brakes to be re-applied. They are also excellent for parking brakes. Most interstate passenger buses and trucks are equipped with some type of safety spring brakes. They are a tremendous investment in safety, and should be installed on every air brake equipped vehicle.

Addition of these spring brakes to an existing system may cost from three hundred to five hundred dollars. Therefore, a bus that is equipped with some type of emergency spring brakes is a better buy than an otherwise equivalent bus without spring brakes. Other types of spring brakes are also available, with minor variations in principle and operation.

As we mentioned earlier, many buses are notoriously under-powered for their size and weight. Don't expect a bus to accelerate as fast nor stop as quickly as an average passenger car. Keep your distance when driving. Don't take chances when starting, passing, or stopping.

Clutches used in some buses are often very stiff to operate, and may be equipped with pneumatic or hydraulic actuators to make operation easier. Synchromesh transmissions are available on later model buses, and are preferred over the older "crash box" or "square-cut" gearboxes. Synchromesh transmissions are much easier to shift either up or down while in operation.

Unlike automobiles, buses are usually designed to last for many years. Many twenty-year-old buses are still in regular service with hundreds of thousands, perhaps even a million, miles. The styling of bus bodies does not change as rapidly as do automobiles. It is usually impossible for the overage person, who is not particularly familiar with buses, to be able to distinguish one model year from another. Some of the neat, modern, converted motor coaches seen on the highway or in campgrounds may be twenty-five years old or more! Age is not the most important consideration. Many of these coaches have been retired from regular public service, and have been renovated and began a new life as a motor coach.

One good source of used buses is local school districts.

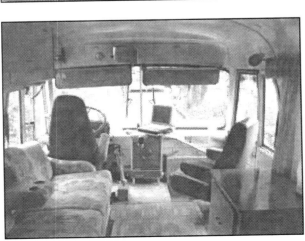

"Giddy-Up Go!" is a 1962 General Motors PD-4106 beautifully converted into a deluxe home on wheels. It has 125 gallon fresh water and 75 gallons each for the gray and black water holding tanks.

It features a full size refrigerator, apartment size range/oven, microwave and 6.5 KW Onan generator.

The bus is complete with a dash-mounted Panasonic laptop with GPS and Delorme Street Atlas Navigational software.

Courtesy of Chris & Lina Toughill

4. Beginning the Conversion

After we have determined what our requirements are, designed our floor plan, and purchased a suitable bus which is reasonably compatible with our plans, we are ready to begin the actual nuts-and-bolts conversion of the bus into a motor coach.

Included with this chapter is a list of minimum tools and equipment recommended for conversion of a bus into a motor coach. These tools should be on hand or available before commencing the conversion.

One problem that often arises is, "where can the bus be parked during the conversion process?" The most logical place, of course, is at your home, provided there is sufficient space to accommodate the bus, and that local ordinances do not prohibit you from doing so. Otherwise, it may be possible to make an arrangement with a local garage, service station, storage yard, etc., to park the bus there while it is being converted. You will need electrical power to operate saws, drills, lights, etc.

The first, and most obvious, step in the conversion of a bus into a motor coach is the removal of all seats, assist hardware, racks, etc., from the interior of the bus. Usually, the seats will be bolted through the floor adjacent to the aisles, and will be attached to angle brackets along each sidewall. Often, the bolts through the floor will be rusted, or perhaps covered with undercoating, making removal difficult. It is often necessary to use a hammer and chisel to cut the bolts loose. The bolts securing the outboard ends of the seats to the angle brackets at the walls are usually easily removed.

Bolts and screws used to fasten and assist hardware, racks, etc., may also be rusted, and difficult to remove. In such cases, it is usually easy to loosen the bolts or screws by placing the appropriate size screwdriver in the slot, and striking the screwdriver sharply with a hammer. The screws can then be easily removed.

Floors in buses are usually either of wood or steel. In either case, the floor may not be flat and smooth, or insulated. It is usually necessary to install some type of insulating, moisture-proof material over the floor, such as Kraft building paper, etc., and install ½" plywood over the entire floor surface. This will give a degree of insulation as well as smooth out irregularities in the original floor. The ½" plywood

sheets should be cut to fit snugly, and be securely fastened to the original floor by means of flat head screws and nuts, with lock washers, or flat-head wood screws in case of wooden floors. Special ring-grooved nails may be used in wooden floors.

Some buses are insulated in both the ceiling and sidewalls, while others may be insulated in the ceilings only, or not at all. It is always recommended that buses be thoroughly insulated for conversion into motor coaches. If your bus is not completely insulated, this is the ideal time to install the insulation.

The interior ceiling and sidewall panels are attached in various ways. Some use sheet-metal screws to hold the panels in place, while others use special channels and metal strips. However, most may be removed without great difficulty.

When the ceiling and/or sidewall panels are removed, the structure should be thoroughly cleaned. It is surprising how much debris collects in the sidewalls of buses used in public service for a number of years. Dirt collects in the sidewalls in particular, and clogs the drain holes located in the lower edge (floor level) of the sidewall. These holes were provided to permit water, running down the outside of the Windows and into the sidewalls, to drain out of the bottom of the sidewalls. However, with the accumulation of dirt, and subsequent clogging of the drain holes, the water is trapped in the lower portion of the sidewalls. In time, rust will eat through the sidewall from the inside to the outside of the bus. Be sure to thoroughly clean the sidewalls and open the drain holes when the sidewall panels are removed. This problem exists primarily in buses that have vertically lowering windows. Newer buses do not have this problem.

Before proceeding further, it is a good idea to lay out the proposed floor plan on the bus floor. This will permit you to accurately coordinate your desired floor plan with the actual layout and dimensions of the bus, and enable you to make any necessary changes in your floor plan to be compatible with the bus.

By laying out the floor plan on the floor of the bus, you may determine which windows will be retained, and which will be closed out. Location of windows in relation to proposed built-ins should receive careful consideration at this time.

Where it is desired to close out a window (or windows), it is recommended that the window be removed, and a strip of plywood, the same height as the window, and of a thickness sufficient that the inside surface is flush with the interior surfaces of the sidewall framework, be permanently installed over the inside opening(s) of the window(s). The exterior of the closed-out windows may be covered with a sheet of thick steel or aluminum riveted or screwed to the outside of the bus. The panel may be primed and painted to match the exterior of the bus.

Where it is desired to install a different type or style of window, the inside and outside should be prepared as above. The new window must be located within the opening of the original window. Locate the new window on the inside wall surface, and trace the outline of the hole cutout. Cut out the opening in the plywood panel using a saber saw.

Measure the space between the plywood panel and the outside sheet metal. Construct a wood frame of this thickness and with an inside dimension approximately 1/8" larger than the window opening. Install the frame in the opening, between the plywood and the outside sheet metal. Secure the frame in place from inside. Drill a small hole through the sheet metal in each corner of the opening. Trace the opening on the outside sheet metal, and cut out using a sober saw with a metal-cutting blade. Install the window in the usual manner. This procedure may have to be varied from one make or model to another, with changes to suit the particular installation.

Where windows are permanently closed out inside and outside, the partitions may be located at any point on the sidewall. Referring to the floor plan again, note the locations of through-the-wall vents, such as the gas refrigerator, water heater, space heater, and ceiling vents. Mark these locations.

Install the insulation in a wall and ceiling areas other than those marked above. The insulation may be temporarily secured in place with masking tape, and will be held securely in place with the furring strips and/or the paneling.

Install furring strips as required to obtain a flat surface for installation of the paneling. Furring strips may be installed to the framework using flat-head bolts and nuts, or self-tapping metal screws.

The electrical wiring may be installed at this time if desired. It is recommended that 3-conductor, #12 AWG copper wire, in accordance with the requirements of the National Electric Code 1968 Edition, be used for all general purpose, fixed appliance, and portable appliance circuits, except for air conditioning circuits. Air conditioning circuits should be No. 10 AWG. (Be sure to check current codes – Editor)

After the electrical wiring has been installed, the interior paneling may be installed. Be sure to make the necessary cutouts for "J" boxes, etc., before attaching the paneling, and draw the free ends of the electrical wires through the cutouts. (8 inches)

Panels may be attached using screws (either wood screws or metal screws, as appropriate) and cabinet washers, or may be cemented in place using epoxy cement. Cemented panels are difficult to remove once the epoxy has set, without destroying the panel.

Wall paneling in the kitchen and bathroom areas may be of Marlite or other similar material, replacing the regular wall paneling in these areas.

Plumbing arrangements in converted buses or motor coaches are dependent upon the type and location of plumbing fixtures installed, the interior arrangement of the coach, and availability of space for installation of water storage and holding tanks. As mentioned earlier, considerable planning is required before beginning the plumbing installation in your coach, It is suggested that you prepare a complete floor plan with right and left side views, showing the location and orientation of all plumbing lines before attempting the installation.
The following is a minimum recommended list of tools that should be available for converting a bus into a motor coach. This list is somewhat flexible, however, and other equivalent tools may be substituted in many cases.

Recommended Tools and Equipment

Mechanic's tools:
- 1 Set ¼" drive sockets, ratchet, and T-handle.
- 1 Set 3/8" or 1/2" drive sockets, ratchet, and T-handle.
- 1 Set combination box and open-end wrenches, ¼" thru 3/4".
- 1 Small ball-peen hammer.
- 1 Medium ball-peen hammer.
- 1 Set drift punches, assorted sizes.
- 1 Set center punches.
- 1 Set cold chisels, assorted sizes.
- 1 ¼" or 3/8" electric hand drill motor.
- 1 Set high-speed twist drills and index, 1/16" thru 3/8".
- 1 Pair pump pliers.
- 1 Pair long-nose pliers.
- 1 Hacksaw and assorted blades.
- 1 Machinist's combination square.
- 1 Pair vice-grip pliers.
- Common and Phillips screwdrivers, various sizes.

Woodworking tools:
- 1 Table or radial-arm saw, assorted blades.
- 1 Electric hand saw.
- 1 Saber saw and assorted blades.
- 1 Set wood drill bits, assorted sizes.
- 1 Bit brace.
- 1 Expansion bit, 1" to 2".
- 1 Smoothing plane.
- 1 Framing square.
- 1 Bevel gauge.
- 1 Hand sander or attachment for electric drill.
- 1 Handsaw.
- 1 Keyhole saw.
- 1 Claw hammer.
- 1 Set wood chisels.
- 1 Set nail punches.
- 1 Countersink bit for drill motor.
- Assorted Clamps, cabinets, C, etc.

Metalworking tools:
- 1 Pair sheet metal snips.
- 1 Blind rivet tools and assorted blind rivets.
- 1 Sheet metal nibbler.
- Assorted metal-cutting blades for saber saw.

Electrician's tools:
- 1 Set of wire strippers.
- 1 Set of terminal crimpers (may be combined with wire strippers).
- 1 Pair diagonal side-cutting pliers.
- 1 Pair electricians' pliers.
- Assorted tape, clamps, insulating material, etc.

Plumbing tools:
- 1 Set tubing benders. (¼" thru ½").
- 1 Pipe wrench.
- 1 Tube flaring set.
- 1 Set hole saws, assorted sizes.

Miscellaneous items:
- Screws, wood and sheet metal, assorted types and sizes.
- Bolts, nuts, washers, assorted types and sizes.
- Nails, common, box, cement-coated, finish, drive-screws, etc., assorted sizes.
- Cabinet washers.

5. Making Interior Contour Patterns

The inside contour of the sidewalls and ceiling in buses varies considerably from one make and model to another. There is no such animal as a "standard" contour, except for the same make and model. Even then, small variations will be encountered.

It is essential that partitions, cabinets, etc., fit the sidewalls and ceiling of the motor coach properly. Poorly fitted walls and ceilings for partitions are a hallmark of an amateur. One of the biggest problems that an amateur faces is making an accurate pattern for the sidewall and ceiling of the bus.

There are several ways this may be accomplished. The first, and simplest, is by taking a large sheet of cardboard and trimming the edges as required, by trial and error, to the approximate shape. A divider may then be used to scribe the approximate contour of the sidewall and ceiling. A more scientific approach is to use a contour layout board.

A 1" x 6" is cut to the exact width of the inside of the bus, at a point at or near the junction of the ceiling and sidewall. The top of a window on each side is a good reference point in many cases. Next, locate the exact lateral center of the 1" x 6". Beginning at the center, and working toward each side, scribe marks across the 1" x 6" at approximately 3" intervals. When within one foot of each side, place the scribe marks closer together, approximately one and one-half inch apart. Use a tri-square or combination machinist's square to scribe the marks accurately

across the 1" x 6".

Using a long ruler or yardstick, measure the vertical distance from the top edge of the 1" x 6" to the ceiling at each scribe mark. Make sure the yardstick or ruler is accurately aligned with scribe mark before making the measurement. Indicate the measurement on the 1" x 6" for each scribe mark.

In case the bus has "cambered" or sloping, curved sidewalls, it is often desirable to determine the exact contour of the sidewalls as well. To do this leave the 1" x 6" mentioned above installed in its position.

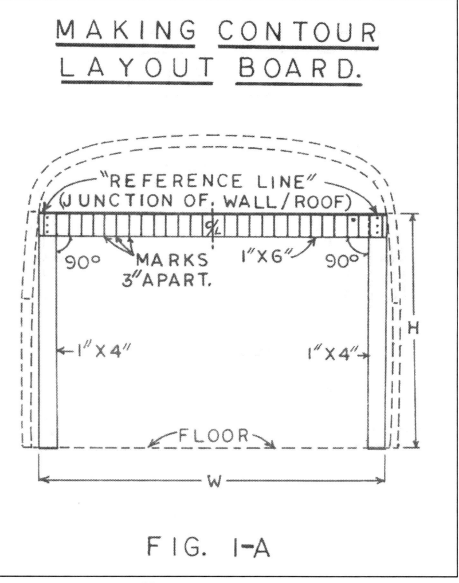

FIG. I-A

Cut two 1" x 4"'s, the same length as the height from the floor to the top edge of the 1" x 6". Attach the 1" x 4"'s to each end of the 1" x 6". Make sure the l' x 4"'s are square (at right angles) to the 1" x 6". A 1" x 2" strip may be attached between the lower ends of the 1" x 4"'s, at the floor level, if desired.

Locate the points of separation between the sidewall of the bus and the outer edges of the 1" x 4". Measure this separation and indicate the measurement on the 1" x 4".

Carefully remove the contour layout frame from the inside of the bus. Place it upon two side-by-side sheets of 1/2" plywood. Again using the yardstick or ruler, reconstruct the curvature on the plywood sheets by measuring the indicated distance from the top edge of the l"x 6" to the ceiling. Again, accurately align the ruler or yardstick with the scribe marks. Make sure the center of the 1" x 6" coincides with the center of the two sheets of plywood. Reconstruct the sidewall curvature by measuring the indicated distance from the edge of the 1" x 4"'s. interconnect the points thus established, and cut out using a saber saw. Thus, you will have a full-face template of the cross-section of the bus, and these will become the master patterns during the construction of wardrobe, bathroom walls and partitions, cabinets, etc. When completed, the patterns themselves may be used as partitions if desired.

It will probably be be necessary to "trim" any panel slightly to ensure perfect fit at any particular point. Bus bodies often vary as much as plus or minus ¼ inch throughout the unit and trimming may be accomplished by use of a block plane, rasp, or sander.

When installing partitions and cabinets, it is recommended that appropriate vinyl molding be installed between the partition or cabinet and the sidewall or ceiling. This vinyl molding is available at trailer supply stores and effectively hides minor misfits.

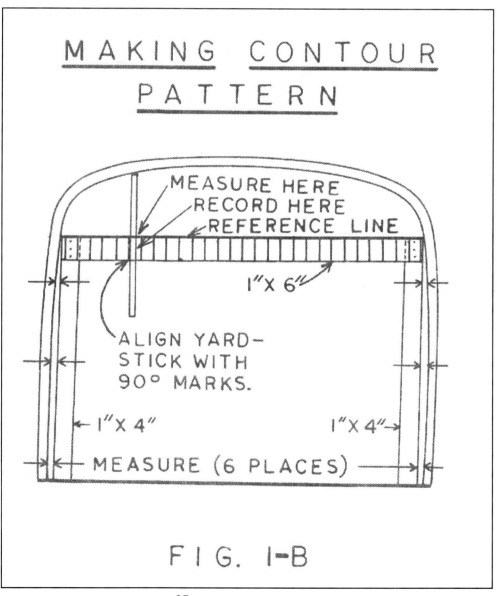

MAKING CONTOUR PATTERN

MEASURE HERE
RECORD HERE
REFERENCE LINE

1"X 6"

ALIGN YARD-STICK WITH 90° MARKS.

1"X 4"   1"X 4"

MEASURE (6 PLACES)

FIG. I-B

MAKING CONTOUR PATTERN

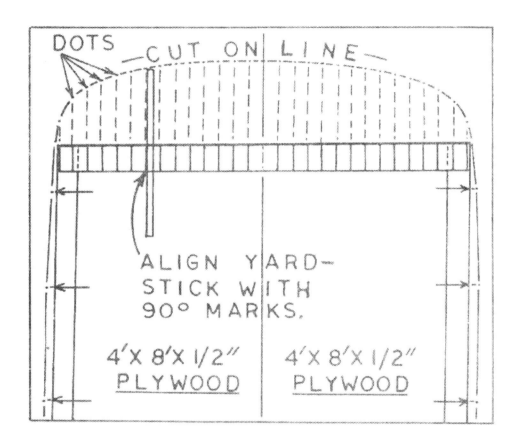

DOTS

CUT ON LINE

ALIGN YARD-
STICK WITH
90° MARKS.

4' X 8' X 1/2"
PLYWOOD

4' X 8' X 1/2"
PLYWOOD

FIG. 1-C

6. Step well Construction

List of Materials:

Ref.	Quan.	Material	Dimensions. (See Drawing)
1	1	¾" Plywood	Width: Overall width less 1½" Height: Overall height.
2	1	" "	Width: Overall width less 1½" Height: .5 (Overall height less 3⅛")
3	2	" "	Width: Width Overall Height: Height Overall
4	1	" "	Width: Width Overall less 1½" Depth: Depth Overall less ¾"
5	3	1½" Angle Iron	Cut each piece to length to fit both sides and rear of stepwell box.
6	7	2" x 4" (1⅝" x 3⅝")	Cut each piece to Overall Width less 1½"
7	1	¾" Plywood	Width: Width Overall less 1½" Depth: .5 (Overall Depth less ¾")

It is often desirable to add an additional door or to relocate the existing door in a bus when converting it into a motor coach. This usually necessitates the cutout of a new door opening, as well as construction and installation of a step well to facilitate easy entrance and exit.

Such a step well may be constructed by following the simple design illustrated in this chapter. Although there are also other satisfactory ways of constructing such a step well, the one illustrated is easy to construct, sturdy, and entirely satisfactory.

As may be seen in the accompanying step well drawing, no dimensions are given, as these will vary with different makes, models, and specific step-well locations. Dimensions will have to be determined from measurements taken from the actual bus for each specific case.

It is usually most convenient to make the new entrance door the same width as the window openings, and to coincide with window openings if possible. Body structural members are normally located in the window mullions, and therefore will not require cutting or relocating when installing a door between the mullions. Likewise, the width of the new door must be compatible with the width of the step well, which will be installed in conjunction with the new door. Therefore, the net step well width (width between the side panels of the step well) should be the same as the door opening.

The height of the step well will be determined by the distance from the floor level inside, to the bottom of the skirt of the outside wall. Floor supporting structure, in the form of 2 x 4's, is located under the step well, and should be included in the overall height. The individual step risers should be equally spaced in the remaining height.

The steps should be approximately eleven to twelve inches deep, which will also determine the overall depth of the step well.

As can be seen in the accompanying drawings, the step well consists of a ¾" plywood box, reinforced with 2" x 4"'s in the bottom and in the step corners.

The individual parts are assembled as shown in the accompanying drawing. It is suggested that marine or exterior type plywood be used, to prevent deterioration due to moisture. The step well should be assembled with screws and glue, and may be painted with a waterproof paint or covered with sheet aluminum if desired. Metal angles, or angle iron may further reinforce the corners, if desired.

The floor cutout should be made approximately one-half inch wider and one-quarter inch deeper than the overall dimensions of the step well box. This is to allow clearance for the mounting angles. The mounting angles should be secured to the step well box by means of ¼" carriage bolts. The angles should be secured to the bus floor by means of flathead screws or bolts.

After the step well is installed, the steps and riser may be covered with rubber non-skid material, or carpeted to match the interior carpeting of the motor coach.

Refer to the Bill of Materials on Page 29 for the key to circled numbers.

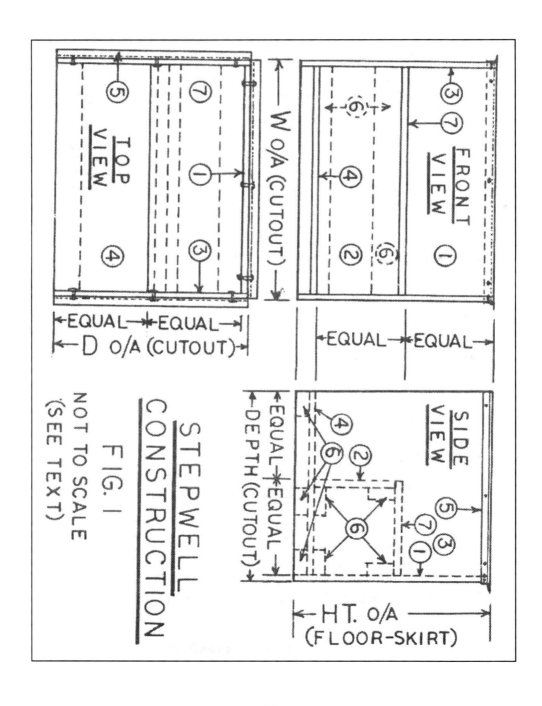

STEPWELL CONSTRUCTION

FIG. I

NOT TO SCALE
(SEE TEXT)

7. How to Build Dinettes

Ref. No.	Quan.	Material	Length	Width
1	2	½ Plywood	Overall Width of Dinette*	20½"
2	2	" "	" " " "	20"
3	4	" "	33 in.	23"
4	4	2 x 4's	11 in.	
5	10	1 x 2's	Overall Width less 1"	———
6	2	2 x 4's	Overall Width less 1"	———
7	2	3/16" Ply. (Prefin.)	Overall Width of Dinette	12½"
8	4	Hinges, 2" x 2"		

*Overall Width of Dinette from wall to aisle.
6d cement coated or box nails.
Glue.
Finishing brads.

The standard dinette is a simple, easy-to-build unit, using standard stock dimension materials and plywood.

All dimensions, with the exception of the width, are given in the drawings or the list of materials. The width is optional. Conventional widths range from 36 to 42 inches for a dinette which seats four adults, and provide sleeping accommodations for two children or one adult. (Wider units may accommodate two adults). An average width of 40 inches is common. The dinette may also be constructed to seat only two persons, in which case the width may be reduced to approximately 24 inches.

The minimum length of the dinette is 80 inches. If space permits, extending the length to 82 inches is recommended. This will provide a bed, which is approximately 74 inches long instead of 72 as in the case of the 80-inch minimum length.

Begin by referring to the list of materials for Construction of the standard dinette. "W" represents the overall width of the dinette, less the prefinished plywood paneling on the aisle side (if used).

Obtain the necessary list of materials, and cut the required number of pieces to the lengths shown in the list of materials. Cut out the plywood end panels, seat and back panels.

Step 1: Glue and nail a lateral strip (5) to each end of the front corner uprights, (4). (Make two rectangular frames). (Fig 1 C/D)

Step 2: Glue and nail a lateral strip (5) along one side of the rear lateral seat support (6). (Fig 1D)

Step 3: Glue and nail the end panels (3) to the rectangular frames (made in Step 1 above) and the rear lateral seat support assemblies (made in Step 2 above). (Fig 1D)

Step 4: Glue and nail the lateral strips (5) between the end panels (3) at the upper and lower rear corners of the end panels (3). (Fig 1D)

Step 5: Glue and nail the back panels (1) to the end panels (3), the upper lateral strip (5), and the rear lateral seat support assembly (made in Step 2). (Fig 1D)

Step 6: Install the seat panel (2) on the bench assembly using hinges. Fig 1C/D

Step 7: Install the prefinished panels on the front of the benches, and on the end panels, **top** strip, and rear of the benches if desired. End **panels**, rear panels and top strip may be upholstered in matching fabric or vinyl to match the interior **decor** of the coach.

Dinette cushions are available in various widths of from 24 to 48 inches as desired. (Other sizes are available on special order). Cushions are also available in 4", 5", and 6" thickness. Dinette cushions are usually made in matching sets, with two of the cushions (seat cushions) normally being 20" wide each, and the back cushions being 16" wide each. A wide variety of fabrics, in solids, checks, floral designs, and vinyl are available in a wide assortment of colors and textures.

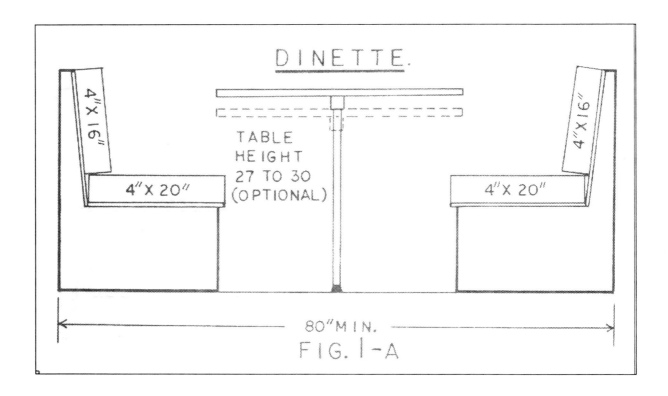

DINETTE.

TABLE HEIGHT 27 TO 30 (OPTIONAL)

4" X 16"

4" X 16"

4" X 20"

4" X 20"

80" MIN.

FIG. I-A

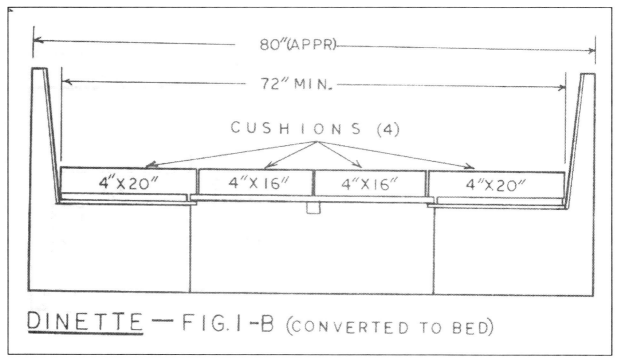

80" (APPR)

72" MIN.

CUSHIONS (4)

4" X 20"   4" X 16"   4" X 16"   4" X 20"

DINETTE — FIG. I-B (CONVERTED TO BED)

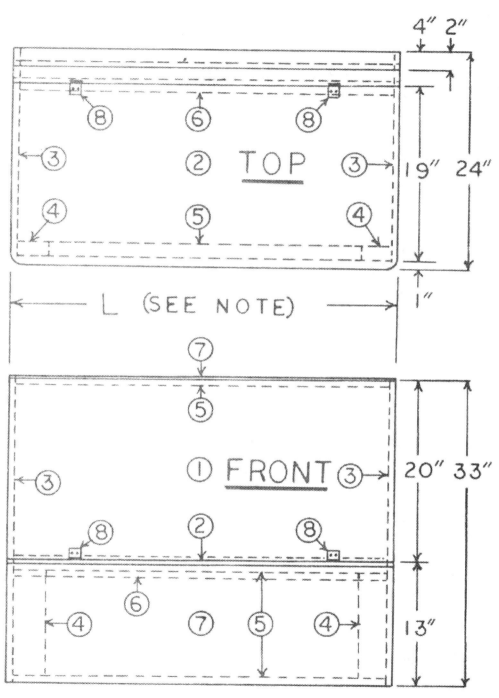

BUILDING DINETTES
FIG. 1-C

Refer to the Bill of Materials on Page 31 for the key to circled numbers.

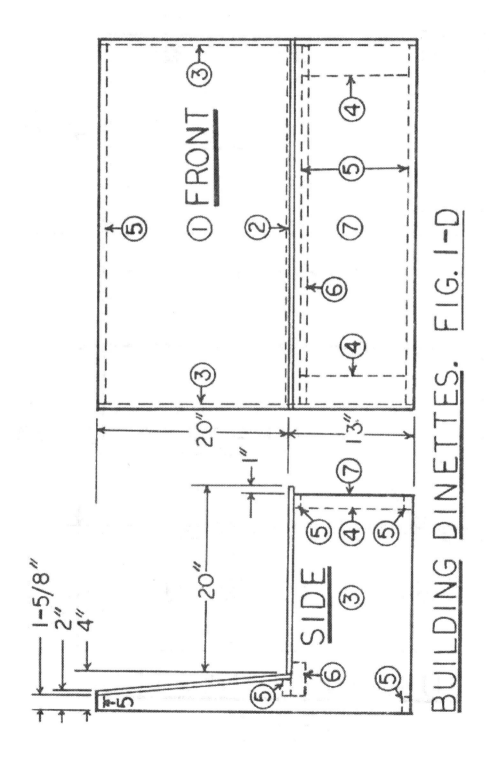

BUILDING DINETTES. FIG. I-D

34

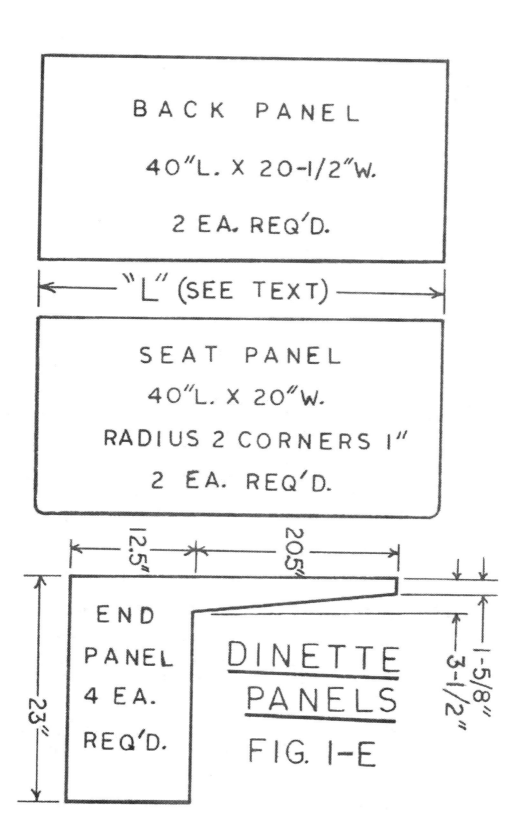

BACK PANEL

40"L. X 20-1/2"W.

2 EA. REQ'D.

"L" (SEE TEXT)

SEAT PANEL

40"L. X 20"W.

RADIUS 2 CORNERS 1"

2 EA. REQ'D.

12.5"   20.5"

END
PANEL
4 EA.
REQ'D.

23"

1-5/8"
3-1/2"

DINETTE
PANELS
FIG. 1-E

Dinette Table

LIST OF MATERIALS FOR THE DINETTE TABLE

Ref.	Quan.	Material	Length	Width
T1	1 sht.	Table topping (Formica, Cono-lite, etc.)	Same as Width of dinette plus ½"	Same as Table Panel plus ½"
T2	1	Plywood, ¾"	Same as Width of dinette	30"-36" as desired
T3	2	Stiffener strips, 1" x 4"	Width of panel less 6"	4"
T4	1	Table Gate Leg	Standard	—
T5	1	Table Bracket Assembly	Standard	—

Note: Alternate swinging table brackets may be installed in lieu of the Gate Leg, if desired. These are available in various lengths, to permit various heights of the table above the benches.

The dinette table is a simple, rugged, detachable table, which may be used in conjunction with the dinette benches to form dining accommodations for four, or may be lowered to form a platform which may be used with the dinette cushions to form sleeping accommodations for two.

Refer to the list of materials required to construct the dinette table. The width of the table may be optional, but widths of from 30 to 36 inches are common. The width may be adjusted to permit the table to fit between the dinette benches, and rest on cleats attached to the front of the benches if desired. This will provide a flat surface for the sleeping accommodations. This often results in a rather narrow table, however. The height of the table may be made to suit, and should be determined experimentally, for greatest personal comfort. The table should extend from the wall the same amount as the dinette benches.

Obtain the necessary list of materials, and cut the required number of pieces to the dimensions indicated in the list of materials. Cut a 3" radius on the aisle-side corners of the table.

Step 1: Glue and screw (or nail) the cross members (T3) to the lower surface of the panel.

Step 2: Attach the mounting rail (T5) to the rear edge of the panel, and flush with the top edge of the panel.

Step 3: Attach the table leg bracket to the forward cross member

Step 4: Determine the desired table height, using 4" thick pads or equivalent on the dinette benches. Cut off the lower end of the table leg to provide the desired height.

Step 5: Install the mating mounting rail to the sidewall of the bus. Be sure the rail is mounted parallel to the floor surface, and well secured to the sidewall structure. The rail should be installed at the proper height to make the table level with the leg-supported end.

Step 6: **Following the manufacturer's instructions**, use contact cement to bond the table top with the plywood, coat the upper surface of the table panel and the lower surface of the topping material generously. Allow air-drying for 30 to 45 minutes, until the cement is no longer tacky.

Step 7: Cover the upper surface of the table panel with heavy, brown wrapping paper. Locate the topping material accurately over the table panel. (The topping material should be cut slightly larger than the table panel to allow for trimming). While holding the table panel and the topping material in place carefully begin withdrawing the brown wrapping paper from between the surfaces. Press the topping material down firmly onto the panel as the paper is withdrawn. When the paper is completely withdrawn, the surfaces should be in complete contact. Use a block of softwood and a hammer to tap the topping material firmly into contact with the panel. **Remember that when the two cemented surfaces come into contact, they cannot be separated or adjusted.**

Step 8: Trim the edges of the topping flush with the panel by scribing and breaking, sawing, filing, or sanding as required. The edge may be finished by applying counter-top edge molding as desired.

Alternate Edge Treatment

If you desire to use "self-edging", i.e., use the same material for the edge of the table as for the top, this edge material should be applied prior to applying the topping material. In such cases, it is common to build up the edge thickness of the panel by securing appropriate thickness wood strips to the lower edges of the table panel. Usually, the edge should be built up to approximately 1-1/2 inches thick. The outside edges should be flush with the edges of the panel.

Cut strips of the topping material 1/2 inch wider than the total thickness of the panel and wood strip.

Place the panel on a flat surface, and raise by means of spacers approximately 1/8 to 1/4 inch above the surface. This will create an even edge around the tabletop on both sides when installing the edging, which can be trimmed for a flush finish.

Following the manufacturer's instructions, use contact cement to glue the edging material to the tabletop. Carefully position the edging material in place, and press

into contact with the edge of the panel. Using a hammer and block of softwood, tap the edging into firm contact with the edges of the panel. Once again, once the edging material and tabletop come into contact, they cannot be separated or adjusted, so use care in alignment.

Trim the edging flush with both the top and bottom surfaces of the panel, then, apply the topping material as directed above.

Refer to the Bill of Materials on Page 36 for the key to circled numbers.

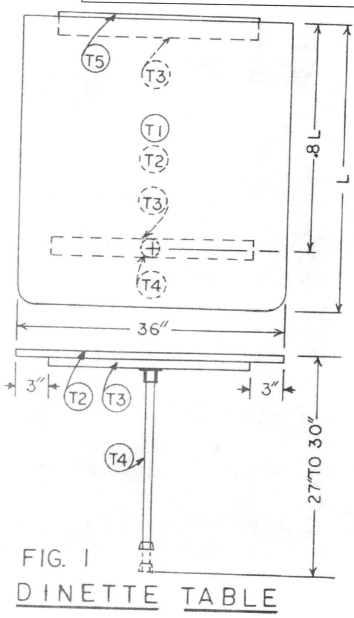

FIG. 1

DINETTE TABLE

Above and inset: In this ingenious dining set-up, the kitchen counter doubles as the dining table. The bench seat folds down for dining and tucks away when not in use, creating more room in the aisle. This disadvantage here, of course, is this setup virtually eliminates the possibility of under-counter cabinets. Courtesy of Steve LaFontaine

Below: A typical convertible dinette. The table leg folds up and locks in place on the bottom of the table. The table is then lowered to create a platform for the seat cushions to form the bed. (Bottom left) Note the drawer at the end of the seat. By carefully designing your floor plan, this drawer can be designed to open up full width creating a large drawer.

Left and middle. This beautiful convertible dinette is easy to use. Simply lift the table and lock it in place against the wall. Then, lift the front of each seat to lower each side into place for a comfortable bed.

Courtesy of KUSTOM FIT HI-TECH Seating Products, Inc.

Bottom left: This photo shows one side of a convertible dinette. Storage for this style of seat would be difficult to access.

Bottom right: A simple, inexpensive storage solution and access is easy if additional sleeping area is not needed

8. How to Build Lounge Bases

The figures detail the design and construction of lounges which may be designed for fixed position as a sofa or single bed, or may be reclined, chaise-lounge fashion, facing either forward or aft. When standard wedge-shaped cushions are installed as a backrest, the lounge is converted into a comfortable sofa, which will seat three or four persons.

The specific design of the lounge, i.e., whether fixed position, reclining facing forward, or reclining facing aft, depends upon the particular location of the lounge, and the individual preference of the owner. The author has installed double-reclining lounges that were installed directly behind the driver and co-pilot's seats, with excellent results. When in the reclining position, facing forward, they afford an excellent view of the countryside. When parked, they may be reclined facing aft, or into the coach, or may be used in the flat position for a single bed.

Figure 1 is a composite drawing of the double reclining lounge, shown in all three positions: the solid lines representing the flat position, the long broken lines representing reclining in one position, and the short broken lines representing reclining in the opposite position. Note that when the lounge is placed in either reclining position, the flat cushion moves endwise approximately 2 to 3 inches. Allowance and clearance must be made for the movement when installing the lounge.

lounge base, which may be used as a single bed, or the lower bunk of a bunk bed set. Note that the top panel is hinged along the longitudinal axis. This offset hinge permits the cushion to slide toward the wall, allowing the top panel to be raised vertically without interference with the cushions.

Any of these lounges may be made any particular length or width, depending upon space available and personal preferences. The top panels should be made of at least 1/2" plywood, however 5/8" or ¾" would be preferred. The side and end panels may be made of almost any suitable material such as plywood, (1/2" thickness and up). The lounges should be firmly secured to the floor of the coach by appropriate means, such as screws, bolts, or other brackets.

Figure 2 shows the top and side views of a double-reclining lounge of the type discussed above. Construction is simplified, and no problems should be encountered during the assembly of the lounge.

Figure 3 shows the end view of the double-reclining lounge shown in Figures 1 and 2.

Figure 4 shows a conventional, non-reclining

One solution to the bed problem is shown here. The lounge table lowers and the couches can be extended to form a huge bed. This works well when the lounge is in the rear of the coach. Amidships lounge/beds would be inconvenient for those wanting to go to the other end of the coach.

Courtesy of Staley Coach

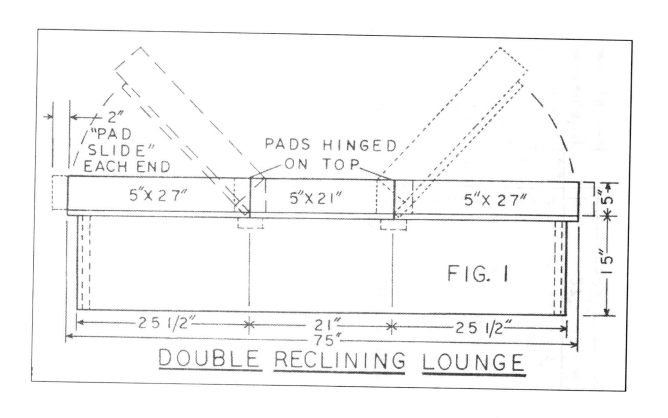

2"
"PAD SLIDE" EACH END

PADS HINGED ON TOP

5"X 27"   5"X 21"   5"X 27"

5"

15"

FIG. 1

25 1/2"   21"   25 1/2"
               75"

DOUBLE RECLINING LOUNGE

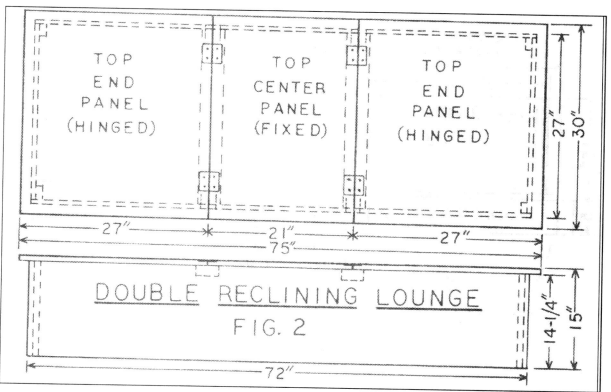

TOP END PANEL (HINGED)

TOP CENTER PANEL (FIXED)

TOP END PANEL (HINGED)

27"
30"

27"   21"   27"
           75"

DOUBLE RECLINING LOUNGE
FIG. 2

14-1/4"
15"

72"

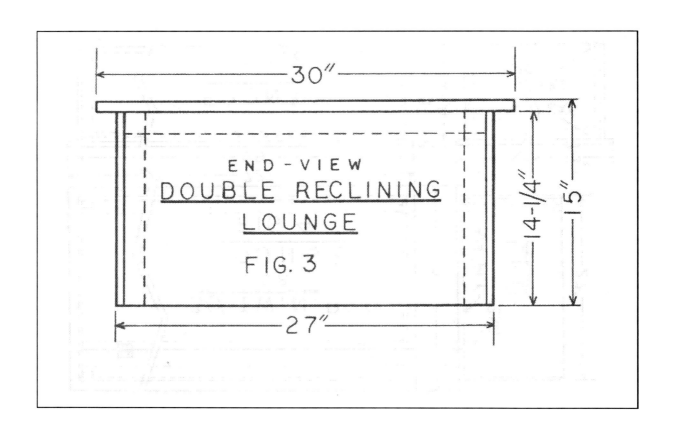

 END-VIEW
DOUBLE RECLINING
LOUNGE
FIG. 3

30"

15"

14-1/4"

27"

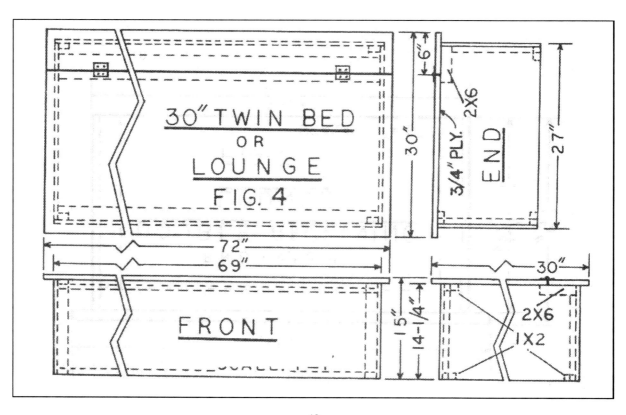

30" TWIN BED
OR
LOUNGE
FIG. 4

FRONT

END

30"

27"

6"

3/4" PLY.

2X6

72"

69"

15"

14-1/4"

30"

2X6

1X2

9. Kitchen Cabinets

There are many possible configurations of kitchen cabinets for use in motor coaches. The standard kitchen cabinets are 36 inches high from the floor to the work surface. For some women, who may be shorter than average height, it may be desirable to reduce this height to 34 or 35 inches overall.

Recessed aisles in some types of buses must be taken into consideration when determining the overall height of the kitchen base cabinets. Recessed aisles usually range from approximately four to six inches deep. The height of the cabinets must be adjusted so that the overall height from the floor in the recessed aisle to the top of the workspace is from 34 to 36 inches. The dimensions given for kitchen base cabinets are for buses with flat floors.

Kitchen base cabinets may be made any desired length to fit the available space. They should be designed to match the interior style and decor of the motor coach.

Counter tops may be made of Formica, Conolite, or other laminates. Counter tops and tabletops should be of the same pattern and color. In general, a motor coach kitchen should provide ample space for the installation of the refrigerator, range or range/oven, and a single or double sink. In addition, there should be as much storage and cabinet space provided as possible, as well as adequate counter space. Many factory-made motor homes suffer from inadequate kitchen counter space.

Drawers for silverware, utensils, towels, etc., should be installed in the kitchen base cabinet. Storage should be provided under the counter top for larger utensils, staple groceries, appliances, etc. A shelf may be installed in the storage compartment under the sinks to utilize the space more efficiently.

Either single or twin sinks may be installed in the kitchen base cabinet. There are special 26-inch long twin sinks available for installation in recreation vehicles, which do not require as much space as the standard 32-inch twin sinks. However, due to the small size of the twin sink basins, they are often too small to accommodate the larger cooking utensils. It is sometimes more practical to install a large single sink rather than the smaller twin sinks.

Wherever practical, it is desirable that kitchen cabinets be constructed with recessed toe-boards. This is not possible with recessed aisle buses. Details of the recessed toe-boards are shown in Figure 1C.

Sink covers may be made from the sink dropout. When these sink covers are installed over the sinks, they effectively increase the amount of counter workspace.

Walls between the kitchen cabinet and the overhead cabinets should be covered with some material such as Marlite, Formica, Conolite, or other similar material. Artificial tile is also used frequently.

Overhead cabinets should be installed over the kitchen base cabinet for dishes, cups, saucers, etc. Hooks may be installed for hanging cups in the cabinets as desired.

Kitchens should be well lighted, both by means of windows and artificial lighting. Most coaches provide a window over the kitchen counter for light and ventilation. Curtains used in the kitchen should be flameproof, and located a safe distance from the range.

Range hoods should be installed over the standard range or range/oven. There should be at least 21 inches of vertical distance between the top of the range and the bottom of the overhead cabinets. The hood should be designed so as to provide at least one-quarter inch of dead air space between the lower surface of the overhead cabinet and the metal top in the hood. Most hoods have a special flange to provide this minimum one-quarter inch air space.

Range hoods should be vented to the outside of the coach. They may be vented by means of a vent pipe extending through the roof of the coach, terminating in a vent cap, or through the sidewall of the coach. Vents should be at least 12 square inches in area. Power vents are also available, containing a filter, blower, and light.

It is suggested that you obtain the necessary installation instructions, including rough-in dimensions, for each new appliance from the dealer or manufacturer, for the particular make and model of appliance which you plan to install. The dimensions are necessary in order that you may make the necessary allowances for the installation of the appliance in the base cabinet. Installation instructions are usually included with each new appliance.

Follow the manufacturer's recommendations carefully when installing appliances. Provide at least the minimum recommended clearances between the appliance and any combustible material. Fasten the appliance securely in place, making sure there is no strain placed on electrical wiring, water or gas lines connected to the appliance. Bond (ground) exposed metal cabinet parts to the chassis of the coach.

Ready-made counter tops for kitchen cabinets may be obtained from local home-building stores, lumberyards, or mail-order catalogs. These counter tops are available in any desired length, and in a wide variety of colors and patterns. They usually have rolled or contoured edges, which makes them very attractive for use in a motor coach.

Counter tops may also be made from 5/8" or 3/4" plywood panels. The panels may be cut to size and secured to the base cabinet. Counter topping is then installed, and the cutouts are made for the sink, range, etc., as required.

Kitchen base cabinets in motor coaches are usually limited to approximately 22 inches wide overall. Standard kitchen base cabinets as used in conventional homes, are approximately 25 inches wide and may be used if aisle width permits. However, standard kitchen cabinets are often used in motor coaches, where the additional width does not materially reduce the aisle width. Standard kitchen cabinets are available in lengths of 42, 54, and 66 inches. They are built so, with the addition of a standard counter top, they will be 36 inches high which is the same height of freestanding ranges, base cabinets, etc. Standard kitchen base cabinets are available in both wood and metal construction. Using the standard kitchen base cabinets is often a fast, easy, economical way to install a kitchen in a motor coach, particularly if wood cabinets are used, which match the interior décor and style of the motor coach.

Refrigerators and iceboxes are available in sizes designed to fit under the kitchen counter. Larger sizes are also available, but must be installed either freestanding or in a special cabinet.

Gas/electric refrigerators must be adequately vented in order to operate properly. Also, they must be installed true to the floor of the coach. Gas refrigerators usually must be reasonably level to operate properly. As in the case of any other appliance, be sure to follow the manufacturer's recommendations regarding installation, venting, etc. Venting may be either through the sidewall or through the roof of the coach, depending upon the size and location of the refrigerator.

Be sure to use the contour pattern you created in Chapter 5 when designing and building your overhead cabinets.

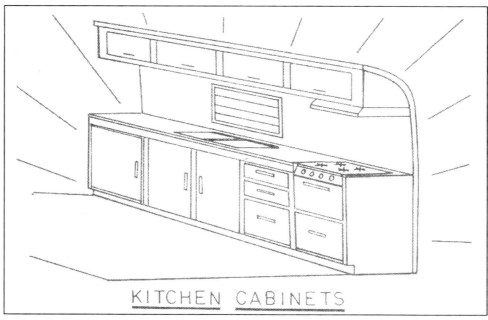

KITCHEN CABINETS

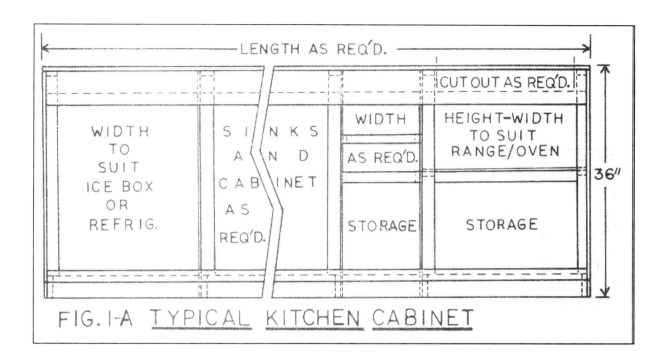

FIG. I-A TYPICAL KITCHEN CABINET

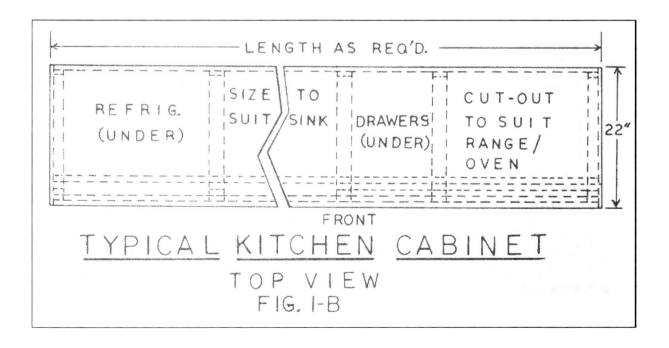

FRONT

TYPICAL KITCHEN CABINET
TOP VIEW
FIG. I-B

45

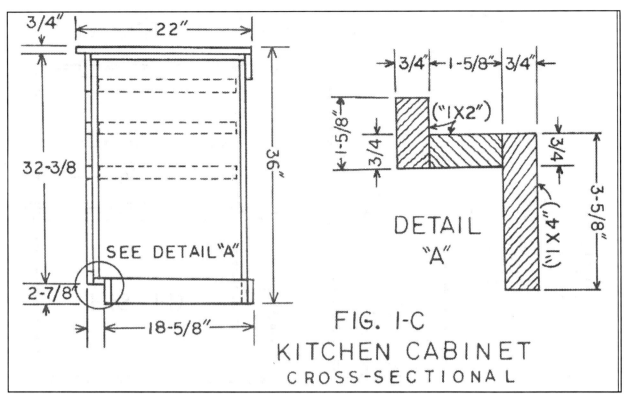

3/4"   22"

32-3/8

36"

SEE DETAIL "A"

2-7/8"

18-5/8"

3/4"   1-5/8"   3/4"

1-5/8"   3/4   ("1X2")

3/4   3-5/8"

("4 X 1")

DETAIL "A"

FIG. I-C
KITCHEN CABINET
CROSS-SECTIONAL

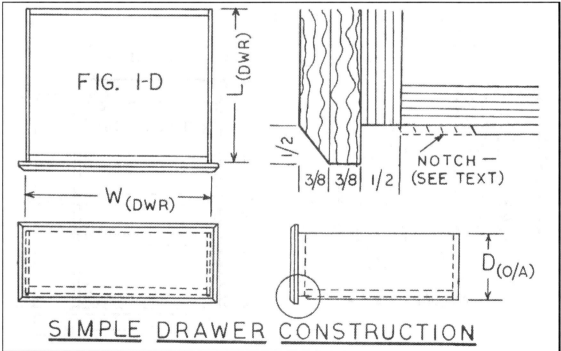

FIG. I-D

L (DWR)

W (DWR)

1/2

3/8 3/8 1/2

NOTCH —
(SEE TEXT)

D (O/A)

SIMPLE DRAWER CONSTRUCTION

Create a small notch (see above) at the bottom of the drawer glides so they will drop slightly when closed to prevent them from opening when the coach is in motion.

46

The minimum distance from the top of the kitchen range to the bottom of the overhead cabinets is 22 inches. The depth of shelves should be between 12 and 16 inches to accommodate plates, etc. One common practice is to make depth to conform to the requirements of the range hood, which will be installed above the range top. However, other cabinets do not necessarily have to be the same size as the one over the range.   Be sure to use the contour pattern you created in Chapter 5 when making the overhead cabinet ends.

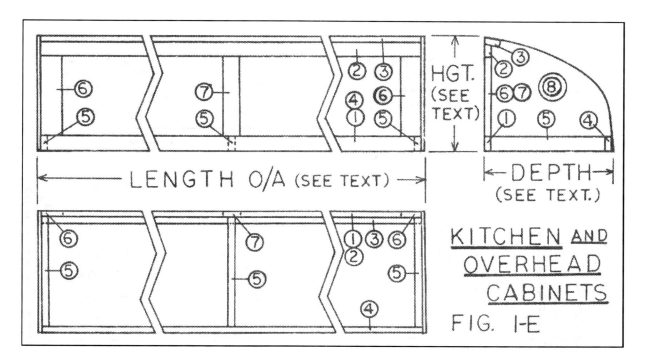

LENGTH O/A (SEE TEXT)

HGT. (SEE TEXT)

DEPTH (SEE TEXT.)

KITCHEN AND OVERHEAD CABINETS

FIG. I-E

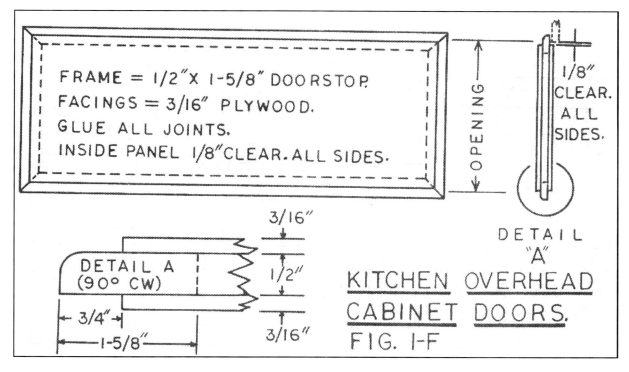

FRAME = 1/2" X 1-5/8" DOORSTOP.
FACINGS = 3/16" PLYWOOD.
GLUE ALL JOINTS.
INSIDE PANEL 1/8" CLEAR. ALL SIDES.

OPENING

1/8" CLEAR. ALL SIDES.

DETAIL "A"

DETAIL A (90° CW)

3/16"

1/2"

3/4"

1-5/8"

3/16"

KITCHEN OVERHEAD CABINET DOORS.

FIG. I-F

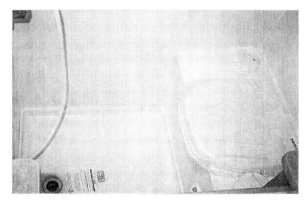

This one-piece modular unit is perfect for smaller conversions. When closed, it provides counter space complete with sink and a 12-volt refrigerator. The right end opens into a one-piece shower and toilet. The shower curtain tucks away on the right side of the unit when not needed. The unit includes its own water pump, a ten gallon potable water supply and an easily removable black water tank. You can plumb the unit to your gray water tank for complete self containment.

Courtesy of Classic Manufacturing, Inc.

48

Many motor home kitchens feature the sink and range on one side, the refrigerator and additional storage on the other.

Above. Another popular option is shown with the dinette opposite the kitchen counter for ease in serving. Unlike most RVs, this kitchen has ample counter space. A portion of the counter space is created by placing a "lift off" counter section over the range's cook top. Some RVs have similar covers for the sink, providing additional working space when the sink is not in use.

Left. The "L" shaped kitchen works well with side aisle designs and when the kitchen is located in the rear of the bus.

Courtesy of Staley Coach

10. Building Bathroom and Wardrobe Enclosures

In Chapter 5, "Making Interior Contour patterns", we discussed a method of making a pattern of the inside sidewall and ceiling curvature of the bus. This pattern will be of use to us when we begin building the wardrobe and bathroom enclosures in our motor coach.

Since the interior dimensions and curvature of different buses vary over such a wide range, we cannot give specific dimensions for the construction of these enclosures. The length, width or depth, and height of the enclosures will necessarily have to be designed to conform to the desired floor plan arrangement, the physical dimensions and curvature of the specific bus which we are converting. However, the framework for these enclosures usually follows the diagrams.

Figure 1 shows a typical design for wardrobe or bathroom enclosures. The base may be constructed using a longitudinal floor member consisting of a 1 x 2 attached at right angles to a 1 x 4 as shown in Figure 2. The end portions of the base may be constructed in like manner. The 1 x 2 may be attached to the floor of the motor coach by use of screws or ring-grooved nails as appropriate.

The upper longitudinal member, which is attached to the ceiling of the bus, may be constructed in somewhat similar fashion, except that the 1 x 4 may be beveled on the upper edge to conform to the angle of the ceiling at that point, and the 1 x 2 may be beveled to provide a flush face for the enclosure.

After the base longitudinal assembly has been secured to the floor, a plumb bob should be used to locate the upper or ceiling longitudinal assembly directly over the base longitudinal assembly. Make sure that the bus is leveled both crosswise and lengthwise before using the plumb bob. This will ensure that the enclosure will be vertical and true with respect to the floor of the motor coach. Attach the upper longitudinal assembly using screws or bolts as appropriate. They should be attached to the roof members or other structure in the ceiling.

End-wall panels may be cut out of prefinished plywood if desired. Use the pattern derived in the Chapter 5, "Making Interior Contour Patterns" as a guide. It may sometimes be necessary to make

minor adjustments to provide a perfect fit.

End-wall panels should be secured to the sidewall and ceiling of the bus, as well as to the framework. There are several methods of achieving this.

The first, and perhaps best method, is to construct a laminated bow from 1/4" plywood strips 1 ½" wide. These strips must be cut uniform, straight and true so use a table saw with a guide rather than cutting them freehand. Use the pattern derived in the Chapter "Making Interior Contour Patterns" as a guide to laying out the jig for making the laminated bows.

To construct the laminated bow, lay the pattern on a ½" or ¾" sheet of plywood. Scribe the sidewall and ceiling contour onto the sheet of plywood. Lay waxed paper over the lines to prevent the laminated bow from sticking to the pattern. Nail short 1-½" thick blocks (6" lengths of 2 x 4 is suggested) around the outer margin of the contour. Bend a strip of plywood to conform to the inside contour of the jig. Secure the strip in place with small nails or clamps. Apply glue generously to the inner contour of the plywood strip. Place another plywood strip inside the first strip, and secure in place using clamps and allow it to dry. Again, apply glue generously to the inner contour of this strip, and install still another strip, etc., until from four to six strips have been installed, providing a bow of between 1" and 1 1/2" thick. Use clamps as required. Allow the glue to set for at least 24 hours before removing from the jig. Construct two such laminated bows for each enclosure (One for each end).

After the glue has set up, the bows may be cut to the proper length, and attached to the sidewall and ceiling using bolts or screws as appropriate. Make sure the outer edges of the bows are flush with the framework of the enclosure.

End-wall panels may be attached to the framework using small finishing nails and glue. The front face of the enclosure may be paneled with a sheet of prefinished plywood, and the openings cut out after the panel has been installed. Use glue and small finishing nails to attach the front panel. If care is exercised in cutting out the opening, the dropout panel may be used as a face panel for the door. This is particularly true where it is desired to align the grooves and match the pattern of the door to the enclosure.

Doors may be either solid core; or laminated.

Stiffening strips may be placed in the door and glued to each panel, to provide stiffening of the door.

Figure 3 illustrates an alternate method of constructing bathroom enclosures.

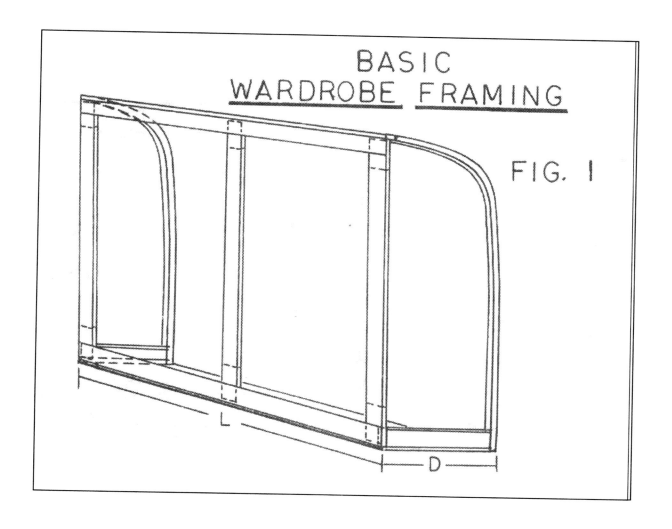

BASIC
WARDROBE FRAMING

FIG. 1

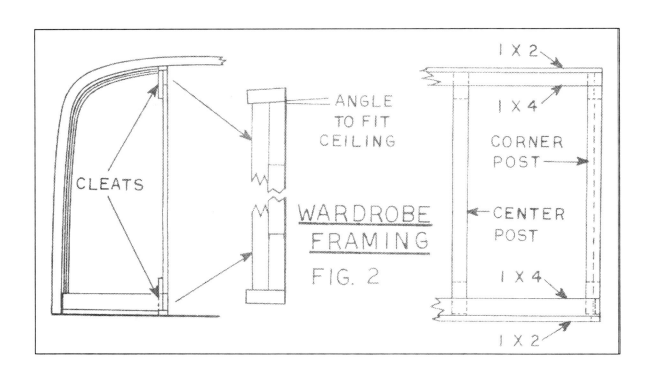

CLEATS

ANGLE TO FIT CEILING

WARDROBE FRAMING

FIG. 2

1 X 2

1 X 4

CORNER POST

CENTER POST

1 X 4

1 X 2

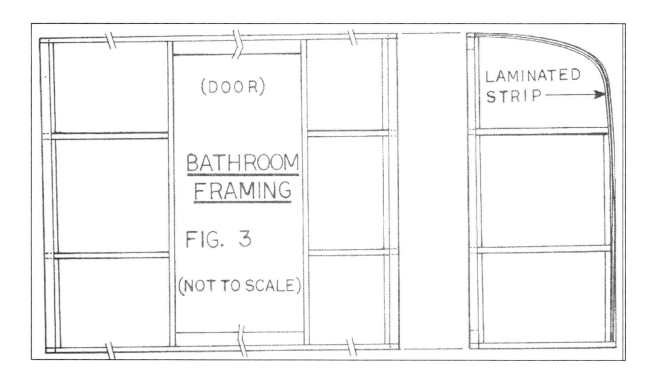

(DOOR)

BATHROOM FRAMING

FIG. 3

(NOT TO SCALE)

LAMINATED STRIP

Laminated Bow Construction

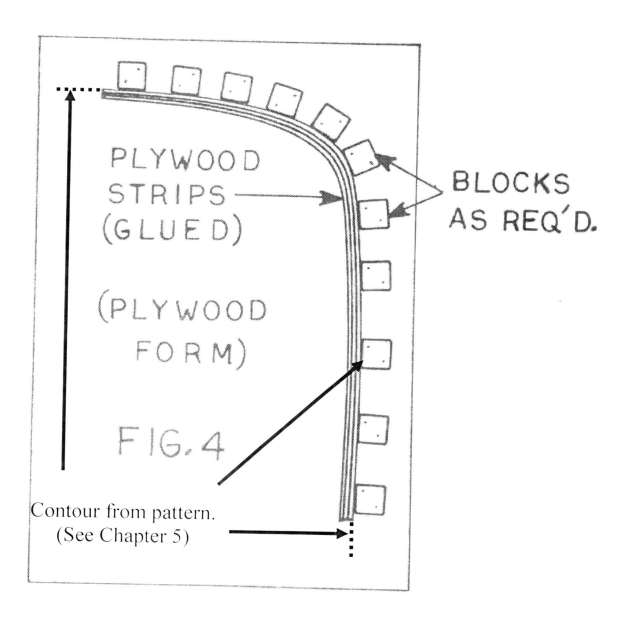

PLYWOOD
STRIPS
(GLUED)

(PLYWOOD
FORM)

FIG. 4

BLOCKS
AS REQ'D.

Contour from pattern.
(See Chapter 5)

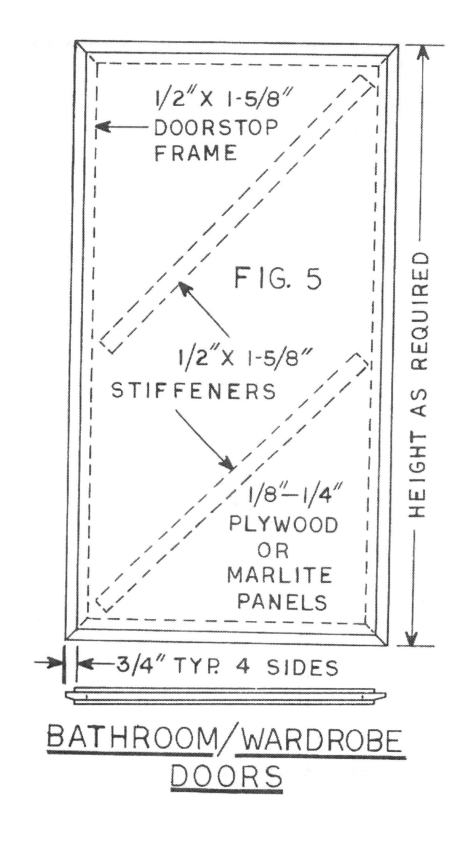

1/2" X 1-5/8"
DOORSTOP
FRAME

FIG. 5

1/2" X 1-5/8"
STIFFENERS

1/8" – 1/4"
PLYWOOD
OR
MARLITE
PANELS

HEIGHT AS REQUIRED

3/4" TYP. 4 SIDES

BATHROOM/WARDROBE
DOORS

11. Self Containment

Self-containment, in a motor coach, is the inclusion of all provisions necessary for complete, independent living accommodations. This usually includes provisions for cooking, refrigeration, hot water, heating, lighting, a water supply, waste holding tanks, toilet, shower or tub, sink, and lavatory. (Definition by the Author.)

Many people construe self-containment to be limited to the inclusion of sanitary facilities only. However, a coach must also have cooking, refrigeration, hot water, heating, lighting, water, and waste holding tanks to be able to operate completely independent of all other sources of power or utilities.

There is a wide variety of types and combinations of fixtures and arrangements for self-containment in motor coaches. It would be literally impossible to list all of the possible combinations and the selection of fixtures and arrangements of self-containment provisions in a motor coach is a highly personal matter.

Most of the fixtures, appliances, accessories, etc., designed for use in recreational vehicles, including motor coaches, have been specifically designed for use in such vehicles. In general, standard fixtures of the type used in conventional homes are not well suited for use in recreational vehicles. All fixtures must be approved by an approved testing agency before they may be installed in recreational vehicles.

The two primary sources of power for motor coaches are electricity and LPG. (Liquefied Petroleum Gas), commonly referred to as Butane, Propane, bottled gas, etc.

In the strictest sense, any motor coach, to be truly self-contained, must contain all the provisions mentioned in the beginning of this Chapter. In practice, however, many coaches only partially meet these provisions. In some cases, complete, true self-containment is not required. Whether or not complete self-containment is required depends to a degree upon how the coach is used. A coach which may be permanently connected to utilities, such as in a park, does not require a water tank, pump, waste holding tank, and may be connected to a natural gas supply. Or, the coach may be entirely electrically operated.

In the current state of the art, a motor coach may be completely self contained using either LPG or electricity as its only source of energy. This energy may come from an on-board electric generating plant (motor-generator set) or from on-board LPG fuel tanks. Most coaches have both — LPG fuel tanks and an electric motor-generator. Most coach owners feel there are certain applications in which LPG is better than electricity, and other cases in which electricity is superior to LPG. For example, most coaches use LPG for cooking, heating, hot water heating, and refrigeration.

Electricity is used for lighting, operation of certain electrical appliances (which cannot be operated by LPG, such as TV, radio, stereo, toasters, coffee percolators, air conditioners, etc.).

Let us digress at this point and discuss some of the various appliances, fixtures, and accessories to be found in a modern self contained motor coach. We shall include those appliances, which require either LPG or electricity to operate, as well as fixtures that may affect the plumbing installations in motor coaches.

COOKING: Most self-contained motor coaches use LPG for cooking. Cooking facilities usually consist of an LPG range or range and oven. The simplest system consists of a two- or three-burner LPG "hot plate". Other units use a combination range/oven, or a three or four burner range with separate oven, usually installed above the range.

REFRIGERATION: The combination gas/electric refrigerator is very popular in motor coaches. These units operate from either electricity or LPG. Newer units can operate on 120-volt AC, 12-volt DC, and/or LPG. They are available in sizes ranging from approximately 4 to 8 cubic feet capacity. When parked in a location where 120-volt AC is available, they may be switched to operate on 120-volt AC. While on the road, they may be switched to operate from 12-volt DC from the vehicle batteries. When parked in remote areas, they may be operated from LPG. This type of refrigerator is very versatile, and is highly recommended for installation in motor coaches. They are offered by a number of different manufacturers.

WATER HEATERS: LPG water heaters are installed in most motor coaches. There are two basic types of LPG water heaters. One is the tank-type, which has a reservoir of from 3 to 10 gallons. A thermostat, operating a main burner, keeps the water in the tank at the pre-set temperature. The other type is the instant hot water heater, which does not have a reservoir. This type has high-capacity burners, which heats the water as it passes through the tubes or coils of the heater. This type only operates when the hot water faucet is opened. Both types are popular in motor coaches.

HEATERS: Most motor coaches are heated with LPG. Thus, LPG is rapidly becoming a universal fuel for motor coaches. Heaters range from approximately 10,000 BTU/hr to 30,000 BTU/hr. Gas heaters may be equipped with automatic thermostats and blowers. All gas heaters must be adequately vented to outside atmosphere, and the combustion chamber must be sealed against fumes entering the coach.

LIGHTING: Both 120-volt AC and 12-volt DC are commonly used for lighting in motor coaches. Some motor coaches are wired with dual wiring systems, with both 120-volt and 12-volt bulbs in the same fixtures. Others are wired for use of 12-volt DC lamps only, which are operated either from a converter (a device which converts 120-volt AC into 12-volt DC) or from the coach's own batteries where 120-volt AC is not available. The modern trend is toward the 12-volt DC system, using a converter and batteries. The batteries may be charged when the system is connected to a source of 120-volt AC, or while driving the vehicle.

WATER SUPPLY: An on-board water supply is basic to self-containment. Most motor coaches are equipped to carry from 20 to 200 gallons of water, depending upon tank capacity. However, water should be used conservatively. The amount of potable water on board, as well as the holding tank capacity, limits the amount of time most motor coaches can be truly self-contained and self-sufficient. As much water as practical should be carried in any motor coach.

WASTE HOLDING TANKS: Along with the amount of potable water on board, the holding tank capacity is one of the limiting factors determining how long a motor coach may operate independently of outside sources. If the kitchen sink, lavatory, shower or tub, and toilet all discharge into the holding tank, the tank tends to fill rapidly,

effectively determining the amount of time the coach may be operated independently. Generally, as much holding tank capacity as practical should be installed.

There are a number of schemes used in the plumbing of holding tanks, and which fixtures are drained into the holding tank. The basic scheme is one in which every fixture empties into the same holding tank. This causes the holding tank to fill rapidly. A better arrangement utilizes two holding tanks, one for the toilet only, and the other receiving the waste from the kitchen sink, the lavatory, and shower. The two tanks are kept separated by means of a separate full-way (waste) valve at the outlet of each tank. The two systems are combined in the drain outlet.

Another system uses a single holding tank, with the kitchen sink, the lavatory, and shower connected to the holding tank. The toilet is of the chemical-recirculating type, which has its own integral holding tank. This system provides greater flexibility in design and plumbing, since the toilet is not plumbed into the drainage system.

The final, and least satisfactory, is one in which waste from the sink, lavatory, and shower are permitted to discharge directly onto the ground, or in some cases, is caught in a container. This raw, untreated waste is undesirable, to say the least.

TOILETS: There are a number of different types of self-contained toilets used in motor coaches today. Some of the more popular types are (1) the mechanical-seal type, commonly referred to as the marine type; (2) the chemical re-circulating type which recirculates liquid waste after chemical treatment; and (3) the non-recirculating chemical type. The mechanical-seal type usually requires a separate holding tank to receive the discharge from the toilet. This often entails additional plumbing. The chemical re-circulating toilet does not normally require an external holding tank, and is completely self-contained. This type often requires a source of 12 volts DC to operate the pump, however. This type of toilet must be serviced (removed and emptied) at frequent intervals. The third type, the non-recirculating chemical type, contains both a fresh water (chemically treated) reservoir and a waste holding tank. Waste is not recirculated in this type. It requires neither plumbing nor electrical hook-ups. This system, like the self-contained recirculating chemical type mentioned above, requires removal and servicing at frequent intervals.

In a slight variation of this type, there are toilets which contain a fresh-water reservoir, a mechanical seal, and a detachable holding tank which may be removed and emptied without removing the entire toilet. All the self-contained toilets, which do not require being connected to a holding tank, simplify installation of plumbing in motor coaches. The choice of a toilet should be taken into consideration when planning a plumbing system.

SHOWER OR TUB: Where space permits, many motor coaches have separate shower stalls or bathtubs installed. Most coaches, however, usually combine the shower with the toilet and lavatory into the same compact space. In larger coaches, or where only two persons will normally be using the coach at one time, a separate shower or tub may be justified. For true self-containment, however, the shower is considered the most likely choice, due to the water consumed by the bathtub. Showers are often the telephone-type, attached to the faucet of the lavatory through a special fitting.

LAVATORIES: Lavatories are included within the bathroom of most motor coaches, although some of the larger units install a separate lavatory outside the bathroom. The lavatory usually presents no problems in plumbing, regardless of whether it is installed in the bathroom or separately.

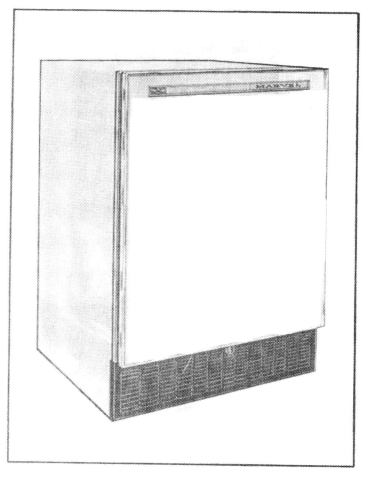

courtesy: Marvel Industries, Inc.
In selecting your refrigerator, consider compactness and design. The size will depend on two factors: the number of people you intend to feed at one time and the amount of available space in your kitchen. Take into account which side the door will open on in order to avoid awkward blockages. Some refrigerators allow the door to be mounted on either the left or right.

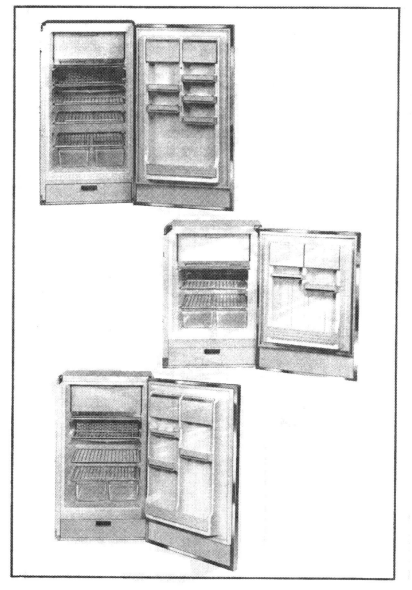

Specially designed RV refrigerators also come in many sizes and design options.
Here are just three available from Magic Chef.

12. Ranges

There are three types of ranges or range-ovens, which are commonly installed in motor coaches. They are the "hotplate", a three or four burner LPG counter-top unit, a three or four burner LPG range with built-in oven and/or oven/broiler, and a three or four burner LPG counter-top unit with eye-level oven.

There are two models of the range with built-in oven. One model is primarily designed for installation in truck campers, and is only sixteen inches overall height. This permits installing the range-oven into the kitchen counter space above the sidewalls of the pickup truck box. However, the sixteen-inch height range/oven, sometimes called the "shorty" is very popular for installation in motor coaches. The compact size of the unit permits greater storage space beneath, or other appliances, such as a hot water heater or space heater, may be installed beneath the unit. This is particularly advantageous for the smaller motor coaches.

The standard twenty-inch high range/oven is usually installed in the larger motor coaches. The unit is essentially the same as the "shorty" model above, except that the oven is approximately four inches higher.

For the larger motor coaches, the built-in range/eye level oven is fast gaining popularity. This unit eliminates stooping when using the oven. Also, the space gained below the cook-top may be used for the installation of a small refrigerator, icebox, gas water heater, space heater, or additional storage. In some converted motor coaches, there may be insufficient ceiling height in the Radiused portion to permit the installation of the eye-level oven.

Ranges or range/ovens are available with or without cook-top burner pilot lights. Most units equipped with ovens have the automatic thermostatic oven control. In some units the oven pilot light remains lit when the oven is turned OFF, while others have a "PILOT ONLY" position which permits the pilot to remain lighted when the main oven burner is OFF. In case of the pilot light extinguishing when the oven is not lighted, the small amount of gas, which would escape through the pilot orifice, would be vented through the rear of the oven. This is not considered a safety hazard.

Hoods should be installed above countertop range units or range-ovens. The eye-level oven type does not require an additional vent hood. Vent hoods should be at least equal to the width of the range, and should cover all flammable material beneath the cabinet to which they are installed. The minimum height between the top of the range and the bottom of the overhead cabinets should generally be at least 22 inches. This minimum height may be reduced to approximately 20 inches if a ¼" inch air space is provided between hood and the underside of the cabinet to which it is attached.

The hood must be vented to the outside of the coach, either with a side vent of at least 12 square inches vent area, or a roof vent of 3 inches diameter. An electrically driven power vent may be installed if desired.

Ranges and range/ovens are normally supplied complete from the manufacturer, assembled and tested. Code requirements often require compliance with the manufacturer's installation instructions for approval of the appliance and installation. Cutout and installation instructions are normally included with each new appliance.

Ranges and ovens designed for RVs come in many sizes and styles. Countertop units and eye-level ovens are a nice option if your ceiling contour makes this possible.

Ranges with top burners and oven/broiler are also popular.

Courtesy of Magic Chef

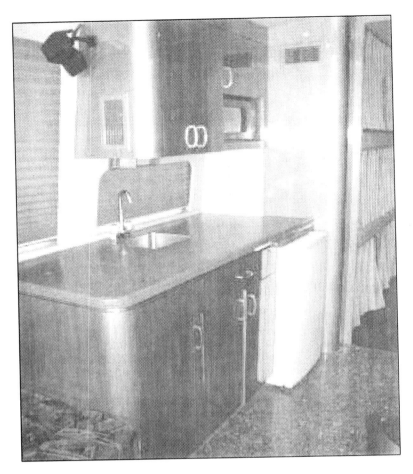

Both of these custom kitchens feature a recessed gas cook top, hidden under a fold-up or removable portion of counter.

The upper kitchen features a built-in under-the-counter refrigerator and overhead microwave.

The lower kitchen includes a separate full-size refrigerator and an overhead microwave convention oven.

As you can see, by recessing the cook top you greatly increase valuable counter space.

Courtesy of Staley Coach

13. Space Heaters

Most motor coaches are equipped with LPG space heaters, ranging from perhaps 10,000 BTUH input for small coaches, to as much as 30,000 BTUH input for the larger units.

The proper capacity heater to be installed in a particular motor coach depends upon a number of factors. First, there is the insulation efficiency of the motor coach itself. Some buses are not insulated. If insulation was not installed during the conversion, they are apt to be more difficult to heat. Likewise, they are apt to be more difficult to cool during hot summer weather.

Floors of motor coaches may be of wood or steel. Steel floors, unless additional flooring, padding, thick carpeting, etc., is installed, tend to be cold and difficult to heat. Wood floors are somewhat better than steel floors in this respect. However, they may be enhanced by in the installation of thick padding and carpeting.

Windows in motor coaches allow considerable heat transfer to the outside unless storm windows are installed.

The severity of winters is also an important consideration. A coach that may be entirely satisfactory in the South or the Southwest may be intolerable in the North and Northwest.

As a rule of thumb, a well-insulated coach should provide a minimum of 12 BTU's per hour per cubic foot of interior space. Therefore, a 30' x 8' x 6' coach interior requires a 17,000 BTUH capacity. If the coach is not well insulated, this requirement may well be doubled.

Space heaters or furnaces installed in motor coaches should be of the vented, sealed combustion chamber type. Combustion air should be drawn from the outside, and combustion byproducts should be vented to the outside. The entire combustion chamber should be sealed against the interior of the coach. This is to prevent gas leaks into the coach, as well as consumption of oxygen from within the coach. DO NOT INSTALL UNVENTED HEATERS IN MOTOR COACHES!

Some States permit the installation of floor furnaces in motor coaches, while other prohibit the practice. Consult your local state code concerning installation of floor furnaces before installing this type in your motor coach.

Furnaces may be forced-air, ducted, or radiant type heaters. The forced air, ducted system is recommended for best heat distribution. For smaller units, a simple blower (less ducts) may be adequate. For the smallest motor coaches, a radiant type heater may suffice.

Some motor coaches may be equipped with trailer-type oil burning furnaces. These units take in combustion air from under the coach, and exhaust through a roof pipe. These units are available in capacities from approximately 20,000 BTU's to perhaps 40,000 BTU's. Most have integral fuel tanks installed.

These units may be installed in a motor coach, and are capable of excellent performance. However, the necessity of having the coach relatively level to obtain proper combustion, and of carrying an additional supply of kerosene or fuel oil, makes them less attractive for motor coaches than the LPG type. Kerosene or fuel oil heaters are slower and more difficult to light than are LPG types, and require much longer to come up to temperature.

There are other motor coaches that use electric heaters that operate from the auxiliary power units (motor generator). These units are considered the least practical, as the motor generator must be operated to provide power for the heaters. (The heaters require too much power to be able to operate on the 30-ampere, 120-volt system).

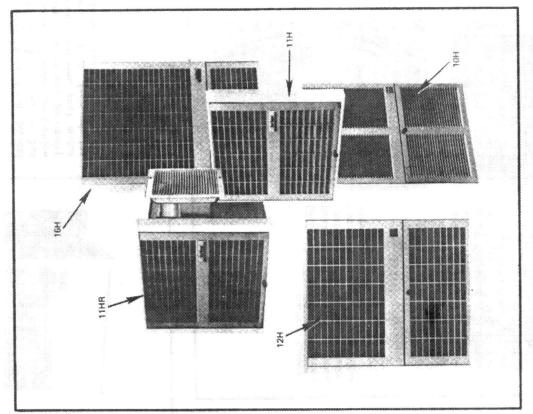

Duo-Therm also manufactures a line of small space heaters with flush venting systems so that there is no protrusion on the outside wall. The largest of these units deliver about 11,000 BTU — far too small to heat any of the smallest conversion units.

courtesy: Duo-Therm

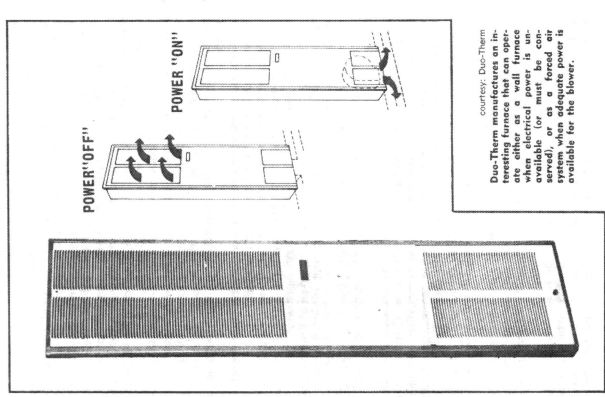

POWER "OFF"

POWER "ON"

Duo-Therm manufactures an interesting furnace that can operate either as a wall furnace when electrical power is unavailable (or must be conserved), or as a forced air system when adequate power is available for the blower.

courtesy: Duo-Therm

Illustrated here is a typical forced air heater for a bus conversion. Sealed combustion system prevents any possibility of fumes entering your motor home. Unit is designed for simple slide-in installation.

Diagrams illustrate Coleman's flexible rear or side venting space heaters. Some installations are far more convenient when side vented.

14. Water Heaters

Fully self-contained motor coaches require the installation of a hot water heater. Water heaters, installed in most motor coaches, can be operated by LPG or combination LPG/120 Volt AC.

For the smallest motor coach, a 3-gallon water heater is available. This little unit requires very little space, and is perhaps adequate for two persons. However, three gallons of hot water do not go very far when taking showers! Even when mixed with cold water at a ratio of 50-50, only six gallons of hot water are available at any one time.

A more practical hot water heater has a capacity of from six to nine gallons. This size is adequate for a motor coach accommodating a family of four.

A recent development in water heaters for recreational vehicles is the combination water heater/space heater. This unit combines a hot water heater with a space heater in one appliance. This may be the answer to the space limitations found in some of the smaller motor coaches.

LPG water heaters must be installed with the vent through the outside wall of the motor coach. The manufacturer's instructions concerning cutout requirements, clearance to combustible materials, etc., must be complied with.

Another type of hot water heater, which is particularly suited for motor coach installation, is the instantaneous-type water heater. In this unit, no reservoir is used. The water is heated as it passes through the coils in the heater. The gas input to the heater when operating is approximately 35,000 BTUH. The heater comes on automatically when the hot water tap is turned on, and continues to deliver hot water until the tap is again turned off.

However, there are always exceptions to the rules. One coach, which the author knows of, is entirely equipped with electrical appliances, and is operated from a 10,000-watt motor generator set. Cooking, heating, hot water, refrigeration, air conditioning, all are operated from the motor generator.

Another unit which the author is familiar with, uses a motor generator to provide power to operate the motor coach, and also provides heat from the motor generator engine to heat the motor coach! This unique arrangement has a small foreign-car engine

installed in the rear to drive a 7500-watt generator. The generator provides power to operate the electrical appliances throughout the coach. The radiator for the small engine is placed such that the heat given off from the radiator is radiated into the coach. An electric motor, driving a fan, is installed behind the radiator to force air through the radiator and into the coach. In summer, valves are reversed, allowing the cooling water for the motor generator engine to circulate through the bus cooling system. Thus, this system uses the motor generator to provide electrical power and heat simultaneously!

Courtesy: Bowen

Bowen manufactures a 6 and 10 gallon water heater designed for recreation vehicles. Unit slips in from the outside to make repair and maintenance easy.

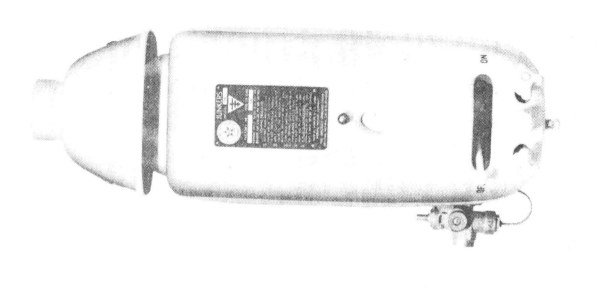

Instantaneous bottle gas water heaters are popular for travel and vacation trailers because their size is small yet they provide adequate supplies of hot water.

Courtesy: Insta-Matic Heater Co.

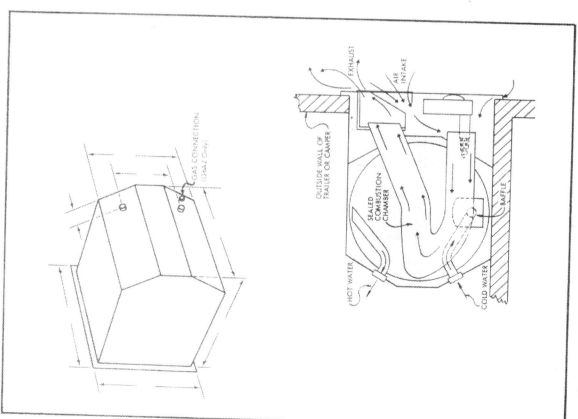

Further details of Bowen water heater shown on previous page.

courtesy: Bowen

15. Plumbing Equipment and Installation

Important note to the 2004 edition:

Many references in this chapter are made to "The Code,"
various tables and the Appendix.
As these references are decades out of date they are not included in this edition.
There are also many "imperatives" in the instructions
using terms such as "shall" "will" and "must".
These references and instructions refer to the
1971 California Administrative code as it relates to RVs.
Use the information in this chapter with discretion
and refer to current codes for your state.

If your state does not have an RV building code, refer to
NFPA 1192 Standard on Recreational Vehicles.
This book is available from the National Fire Protection Association
http://www.nfpa.org   Enter "1192" in the search box.

If your conversion does not meet these standards,
you may be unable to register/insure your conversion.

General Requirements.

The following general requirements apply to both drainage systems and water distribution systems.

1. All exterior openings around piping shall be sealed to prevent ingress by rodents.

2. No drainage or vent piping shall be drilled or tapped for the purpose of making connections. Except as provided in this chapter, no vent pipe shall be used as a waste or drainpipe. No equipment or installation that obstructs or retards the flow of water, waste, sewage, or air in the drainage or vent system in an amount greater than the normal frictional resistance to flow shall be used. Cracks, holes, or other imperfections in equipment shall not be concealed by welding, brazing, or soldering or by paint, wax, tar, or other leak sealing or repairing agents. Equipment shall be located so as not to interfere with the normal use or operation of windows, doors, or required facilities. Galvanized pipe shall not be bent or welded. All valves, pipes, and fittings shall be installed in correct relationship to the direction of flow.

3. Standards for equipment and installations are listed in Table 51. (Refer to Appendix). Products conforming to these standards shall be considered acceptable by the department, when installed in accordance with the provisions of this chapter and the conditions of their approval, except where otherwise provided in this chapter. (The Appendix is obsolete and not included in this work. – Editor)

4. Piping in a plumbing system shall be installed so that it will not be subject to undue strains and stresses. Provision shall be made for expansion and contraction. Piping shall be securely attached to the structure by proper hangars, clamps, or brackets which provide protection against motion, vibration, road shock, torque in the chassis, or other usual conditions. Hangars and anchors shall be of sufficient size and strength to support their proportional shore of the pipe and prevent vibration. Unless otherwise required, piping shall be secured at four-foot intervals, or less, to keep the pipe in alignment and carry the weight of the pipe and contents.

5. Joints and connections in the plumbing system shall be gas tight and watertight for the pressures required under testing procedures. Pipe threads and

slip joints shall not be wrapped with string, putty, or similar fillers. Threads for screw pipe and fittings shall conform to the approved or listed standard. All burrs shall be removed. Pipe ends shall be reamed out to size of bore, and all chips shall be removed. Pipe joint cement or thread lubricant shall be applied to male threads only. Pipe threads shall be fully engaged with the threads of the fitting.

Solder joints for tubing shall be made with sweat solder-type fittings. Surfaces to be soldered shall be cleaned bright. The joints shall be properly fluxed with non-corrosive-type flux and made with 50-50 solder or solder having a higher melting temperature. Copper tubing shall be inserted to the full depth of the solder cup. Plastic pipe and fittings shall be joined by approved installation methods. Plastic pipe shall be inserted to the full depth of the welding socket of the fitting.

Drainage Systems

1. Drainage piping shall be standard weight steel, wrought iron, brass, copper tube DWV, ABS plastic, or other approved or listed materials as per section 23010 of this article. (Refer to Appendix). (The Appendix is obsolete and not included in this work. – Editor)

2. Drainage fittings shall be recessed drainage pattern, with smooth interior waterways of the same diameter as the piping and shall be of a material conforming to the type of piping used. Drainage fittings shall be designed to provide for a one-fourth inch per foot grade. Fittings for screw pipe shall be cast iron, malleable iron, brass, or ABS plastic with standard pipe threads. Fittings for copper tubing shall be cast brass or wrought copper. Fittings for plastic piping shall conform to the requirements of section 23712 (See Appendix). Brass adapter fittings shall be used to join copper tubing to threaded pipe. (The Appendix is obsolete and not included in this work. – Editor)

Drain Outlets

1. A recreational vehicle having a mechanical seal toilet with a waste holding tank or a recirculating chemical toilet may have a separate drain which may be located at any location on the perimeter of the vehicle within 18 inches of the outside wall and shall be provided with a full-way valve. The drain for the remainder of the plumbing system shall be considered the main drain.

The full-way valve shall be provided with a standard three inch male thread and female threaded

cop which is securely fastened to the vehicle and shall not be equipped with extensions or other actuating devices or be installed in such a manner than discharge may be accomplished while the vehicle is in motion.

A vehicle designed to be used with motive power, or a recreational vehicle not over 17 feet in length, may have the main drain outlet located on either the road or curb side, provided the combination LP-natural gas, water and electrical connections are located on the same side or rear as the main drain.

2. Drain outlets shall be equipped with a watertight cap or plug, which shall be permanently attached to the vehicle.

3. The drain outlet and couplers shall be provided with a minimum clearance of three inches in any direction from all parts of the structure or appurtenances and with not less than 18 inches unrestricted clearance directly in front of the drain outlet.

4. Drain couplers for drain outlets shall be a quick-disconnect type not requiring any special tools or knowledge to make the connection or remove the drain hose. Drain couplers shall not be smaller than the piping to which they are connected.

5. The drain outlet and attached drain coupler for a vehicle equipped with a toilet shall be three-inch minimum inside diameter.

6. However, the main drain for a recreational vehicle having a separate drain, as described in (1) above, shall not be less than one and one-half inch minimum inside diameter. (This paragraph applies only when the toilet does not dump into the holding tank or drain through the drain outlets).

Size of Drainage Plumbing

1. Drainage pipe sizes shall be determined by the type and number of fixtures connected to each drain. One and one-half inch minimum diameter piping shall be required for one and not more than three individually vented fixtures. A two-compartment sink or two single sinks or two lavatories set immediately adjacent to each other in the same room with the waste outlets not more than 30 inches apart may be connected to one trap and may be considered as one fixture. Two-inch minimum diameter piping shall be required for four or more fixtures individually vented. Three-inch minimum diameter piping shall be required for

toilets.

2. Plumbing fixture traps may connect into a wet-vented drainage system, which shall be designed and installed to accommodate the passage of air and waste in the same pipe. All parts of a wet-vented drainage system, including the connected trap arms, shall be horizontal except for wet-vented vertical risers which shall terminate with one and one-half-inch minimum diameter continuous vent. Where required by structural design, wet-vented drainage piping may be offset vertically when other vented trap arms or relief vents are connected to the drainage piping below the vertical offsets. A wet-vented drainage pipe shall be at least one pipe size larger than the largest connected trap arm. Not more than three fixtures may connect to a wet-vented drainage system. A waste holding tank vent may serve as a drain from one additional fixture, providing the pipe is increased one pipe size from the tank to the fixture tee.

3. A recreational vehicle that has no plumbing fixtures connected to the main drain other than a one or two compartment kitchen sink, with drain openings of not more than two inches in diameter, may be connected to a side vent drainage system. Side-vent drainage systems shall be constructed of one and one-fourth-inch minimum diameter, Schedule 40, material listed in section 23712 (See Appendix) or one and one-half inch outside diameter drawn brass tubing of not less than No. 20 Brown and Sharpe gauge with drawn or cast brass fittings. The drain outlet size shall be one and one-half-inch diameter. Traps shall be one and one-fourth-inch minimum diameter installed as close to the sink as possible with the center of the outlet not more than six inches from the bottom of the sink. An approved baffle or diverter tee shall be used to connect the trap arm to the vertical drain and vent. The center of the elbow on the vent offset through the outside wall shall not be less than two and one-fourth-inches above the bottom of the sink. The drain may terminate through the outside wall above the floor or extend vertically through the floor to the exterior.

Offsets and Branch Drainage Fittings

Changes in direction of drainage piping shall be made by the appropriate use of fittings of 11 1/4, 22 1/2, 45 or 60 degrees, or other fittings or combinations of fittings with equivalent sweep.

Horizontal drainage lines, connecting with a vertical pipe, shall enter through 45-degree Y branches, long-turn TY branches, sanitary I branches, or other fittings or combination of fittings having equivalent sweep. No fitting having more than one branch at the same level shall be used, unless the fitting is constructed so that the discharge from any one branch cannot readily enter any other branch. However, a double sanitary tee may be used when drainage line is increased not less than two pipe sizes.

Horizontal drainage lines connecting with other horizontal drainage lines, or vertical drainage lines connected with horizontal drainage lines, shall enter through 45-degree Y branches, long-turn TY branches, or other fittings or combination of fittings having equivalent sweep.

Horizontal drainage piping shall be run in practical alignment and have a uniform grade of not less than one fourth inch per foot toward the vehicle drain outlet. Where it is impractical to obtain a grade of one-fourth-inch-per-foot because of structural features or arrangement of any vehicle, the pipe or piping may have a grade of not less than one-eighth-inch-per-foot, provided a full-size clean out is installed at the upper end.

Vehicles equipped with a waste-holding tank and a toilet shall have a mechanical seal or recirculating chemical toilet. Connections shall be three-inch minimum pipe size and shall extend downward into the tank sufficiently to maintain a high water level clearance below the top opening. Drain opening shall be a three-inch minimum pipe size outlet located at the lowest point in the tank and shall be fitted with a full-way valve. Full-way valves referred to in subsection (b) (See Appendix) shall be designed for manual operation from outside the vehicle and shall have no extension or activating device within the unit.

The (holding) tank shall be vented by one of the following methods:
(1) A one and one-fourth-inch minimum diameter individual vent pipe extending undiminished in size through the roof;

(2) Two or more vented drains when at least one is wet-vented and each drain is separately connected to the top of the tank: or
(3) The waste holding tank vent may serve as a drain from one additional fixture, providing the pipe is increased by one pipe size larger than the connected trap or trap arm.

Waste holding tanks shall be securely installed in such locations as to be removable for service, repair, and replacement, without the necessity of removing permanent structural, mechanical, or electrical installations.

Traps and Cleanouts

1. Each plumbing fixture shall be individually trapped by a water seal P-trap, except as permitted in section 23772 (See Appendix), except for recirculating chemical and mechanical seal toilets. Toilets, except recirculating chemical and mechanical seal types, shall have integral traps. All traps shall be effectively vented. Only one trap shall connect to a trap arm.

2. A two-compartment sink, two single sinks, or two lavatories set immediately adjacent to each other in the same room with waste outlets not more than 30 inches apart may be connected to one trap and may be considered as one fixture for the purpose of drainage and vent requirements.

In a recreational vehicle, two single sinks, two lavatories, or a single sink and a single lavatory with waste outlets not more than 30 inches apart, may be connected to one trap for the purpose of drainage and vent requirements when an approved fixture diverter tee is used. Note: For recreational vehicles, it is not required that the two fixtures be in the same room, provided the waste outlets are not more than 30 inches apart.

No form of trap, which depends, for its seal upon concealed interior partitions shall be used. Full S traps, bell traps, drum traps, and crown-vented traps are prohibited, and no fixture shall be double-trapped.

Each trap shall be self-cleaning with a smooth and uniform interior waterway. Traps shall be manufactured of cast iron, cast brass, or drawn brass tubing of not less than No. 20 Brown and Sharpe gauge, ABS plastic, or other approved or listed material. Union points for a trap shall be beaded or beveled to provide a shoulder for the union nut. Each trap shall have the manufacturer's name stamped or cast on the surface of the trap, and each tubing trap shall also show the gauge of the tubing.

Each trap shall have a water seal of not less than two inches and not more than four inches and shall be set true to its seal.

Traps shall not be less than one and one-half-inches

in diameter, except that one and one-fourth-inch diameter trap may be used when connected to a single fixture having no more than a two-inch drain opening. No trap shall be larger than the waste pipe to which it is connected.

Each trap shall be located as close to its vent and to the fixture outlet as structural conditions will permit.

The distance between a trap and its vent or vented waste line shall be not more than shown in Table 52 in section 23841 of the Code. (The "Code" is obsolete and not included in this work. – Editor)

The vertical distance from a trap to the fixture outlet shall not exceed 24 inches.

Traps: Installation

The trap arm between a trap and the fixture tee or the vented waste line shall be graded one-fourth-inch-per-foot towards the vent and in no event shall have a slope greater than its diameter. Except for toilet drains, the vent opening at fixture tees shall not be below the invert of the trap Outlet.

The trap arm between the trap and vent may change direction or be offset horizontally with the equivalent angle of not more than 180 degrees.

Traps with slip-joint connections shall be accessible for repair and inspection.

Traps shall be designed and installed so they can be separated by the use of a mechanical joint.

Cleanout Openings

Clean-outs shall be provided in the drainage system when other convenient and adequate means for cleaning the system are not provided. It shall not be considered convenient and adequate means whenever it is necessary to remove any pipe, fixture, or fitting in order to remove a stopping in the system. In accordance with section 23763, of this chapter (See Appendix) a full size clean-out shall be installed at the upper end of any section of drainage piping which does not have the required minimum slope of one fourth inch per foot grade. A cleaning tool shall not be required to pass through more than 360 degrees of fittings to reach any part of the drainage system. **(The Appendix is obsolete and not included in this work. – Editor)**

Clean-outs shall be accessible through an

unobstructed minimum clearance of 12 inches directly in front of the opening. Each clean-out fitting shall open in a direction opposite to the flow or at right angles to the pipe. Concealed clean-outs that are not provided with access covers shall be extended to a point above the floor or outside the vehicle with pipe and fittings installed, as required, for drainage piping.

Plugs and caps shall be brass or plastic, with screw pipe threads.

Clean-out plugs shall have raised heads except that plugs at floor level shall have counter-sunk slots.

Vents and Venting

Each plumbing fixture trap shall be protected against siphonage and backpressure, and air circulation shall be ensured throughout all parts of the drainage system by means of vent pipes.

Vent piping shall be standard weight steel, wrought iron, brass, copper tube DWV, and ABS plastic or other approved or listed materials, pursuant to section 23712 of this chapter (See Appendix). (The Appendix is obsolete and not included in this work. – Editor)

Appropriate fittings shall be used for all changes in direction or size and where pipes are joined. The material and design of vent fittings shall conform to the type of piping used.

Fittings for screw pipe shall be cast iron, malleable iron, brass, or ABS plastic with standard pipe threads.

Fittings for copper tubing shall be cast brass or wrought copper.

Fittings for plastic piping shall conform to the requirements of section 23712 of this chanter. (See Appendix.) (The Appendix is obsolete and not included in this work. – Editor)

Brass adapter fittings shall be used to join copper tube to threaded pipe.

The drain piping for each water flush toilet shall be vented by a one and one-half-inch minimum diameter vent connected to the main drain by one of the following methods:

1. A one and one-half-inch diameter individual vent pipe directly connected to the toilet drain and

extending undiminished in size through the roof.

2. A one and one-half-inch minimum diameter continuous vent indirectly connected to the toilet drain piping through a two inch wet-vented drain that carries the waste of not more than one fixture, or not more than two fixtures when one is a combination compartment drain;

3. Two or more vented drains when at least one is wet-vented and each drain is separately connected to the main drain.

When the toilet, other than a recirculating chemical toilet, is located in a shower stall that is limited to 12 square feet or less in floor area, the trap branch from the shower drain may be directly connected to the toilet drain piping without any additional venting.

A one and one-fourth-inch minimum diameter vent pipe shall be required for all individually vented fixtures with one and one half-inch or smaller traps. The main vent, toilet vent, relief vent, and the continuous vent of wet-vented drainage systems shall be one and one-half-inches in diameter.

A recreational vehicle having a main drainage system installed in accordance with Paragraph 1 (DRAIN OUTLETS), may have a vent one-pipe size smaller than the main drain.

When two fixture traps located within the distance allowed from their vent have their trap arms connected separately at the some level into a double fitting, an individual vent pipe may serve as a common vent without any increase in size.

Where two or more vent pipes are joined together, no increase in size shall be required; however, the largest vent pipe shall extend full size through the roof and shall be not less than one and one-half-inch in diameter. The developed length of a trap arm from the weir of the trap to the inner edge of the vent shall be within the distance shown in Table 52. (See Appendix.)

Waste Plumbing

The waste plumbing systems in motor coaches may vary from the simplest to the most complex arrangements. Factors determining the degree of simplicity or complexity of the waste plumbing system are (1) the number and type of fixtures installed; (2) the degree of self-containment desired; and (3) the physical arrangement of the plumbing fixtures, equipment, etc.

Regardless of the arrangement, however, there are certain standards governing the installation of fixtures and waste plumbing, which must be complied with. Among these are (1) the use of approved fixtures; (2) the use of approved materials; and (3) the method of installation.

All fixtures and materials used in the waste plumbing system must be approved for such use by a recognized testing agency. In addition, they must be installed in accordance with existing applicable codes and the manufacturer's specific instructions. Many states have adopted codes governing the installation of plumbing fixtures and equipment in mobile homes, travel trailers, motor homes, and campers. In such case, it is advisable to comply with those codes as applicable. However, in the absence of such codes, we have included applicable excerpts from the California Administrative Code, Title 8, Industrial Relations, Part 2, Department of Housing and Community Development, Chapter 4, Plumbing, Heat-Producing and Electrical Equipment in Mobile homes. This code is perhaps typical or representative of those adopted by other states.

Included in Table 51 of the above-mentioned California Administrative Code (see Appendix) is a list of applicable standards for plumbing fixtures and materials, as well as standards for the installation of these fixtures and materials. All fixtures, materials, and installations should be in conformance with these standards. Fortunately, most of the fixtures and materials offered by major manufacturers and suppliers of equipment for motor coaches are in conformance with these standards. It is not sufficient that the fixtures and materials be approved for the particular application, but also the installation must be in accordance with the code and the manufacturer's instructions

Also, included in this chapter; are simplified drawings and schematics of typical waste plumbing systems.

Many motor coaches are now using self-contained chemical toilet systems, which do not require the installation of a separate holding tank to receive the discharge from the toilet. These devices greatly simplify the installation of holding tanks and drainage systems and allow much greater flexibility in design of the system. These self-contained chemical toilets must be removed from the motor coach at frequent intervals and dumped info an external sewerage system. There are also other types of toilets, which evaporate the waste by means of burning or heating by LPG or the engine exhaust systems.

Most motor coaches have, as a minimum, a one-or-two compartment kitchen sink, a lavatory, toilet, and shower. As mentioned above, the toilet may be connected to the holding tank system, or may be a self-contained chemical type. For smaller motor coaches, or those with small holding tanks, it is often advisable to use the self-contained chemical toilet instead of the conventional type.

Many motor coaches, both factory-made and converted units, do not have holding tanks installed. Instead, the kitchen sink waste, the lavatory waste, and the shower waste are either connected to a sewer system when sewer facilities are available, or are caught in an external pail and periodically emptied as required, or are allowed to empty on the ground. The latter methods are not recommended. In the interest of sanitation and ecology, it is preferable to install a holding tank to receive the waste from these sources and dump them into an external sewer system. Many service stations, parks, motor home sales lots, etc., have facilities for dumping holding tanks.

Consider first the proper method of installing the waste plumbing system for a two-compartment kitchen sink.

Standard basket strainers are installed in each sink. These are connected together by means of a continuous Waste assembly. The continuous waste assembly in turn is connected to a standard 1 1/2" "P" trap. The "P" trap may be either cost iron, cast brass, drawn brass tubing (No. 20 Brown and Sharp gauge) ABS plastic, or other approved material. The "P" trap is in turn connected to a 1 1/2" horizontal trap arm. The trap arm is also 1 1/2" diameter, and no more than 4'6" in length. It should extend directly to the vent pipe. The horizontal trap arm should have a slope, or grade, of approximately 1/4" per foot of length. It should connect to the vertical vent by means of a 2" -x 1 1/2" x 1 1/2" "sanitary tee".

The upper portion of the vent should be also of 1 1/2" ABS plastic pipe, and should continue undiminished in size through the roof of the motor coach. Vertical offsets may be made by use of appropriate vent (short-turn) fittings. The vent pipe should extend 3" above the roof. The opening around the vent should be sea led with appropriate roof jocks or flashing.

Next, consider the proper method of installing a toilet to a holding tank. In this case, the holding tank is installed below the floor surface. The illustration represents a recessed-shower pan, and pedestal-mounted toilet. The shower pan acts as the floor for the bathroom. The toilet is elevated 4" with respect to the floor of the bathroom. Special "shorty" toilets are available which maintain the proper overall height from the floor to the toilet seat.

The toilet may be mounted at any point on the top surface of the holding tank. The holding tank is fitted with a 3" opening to accept the 3" pipe from the bottom of the toilet. The pipe between the bottom of the toilet and the holding tank must be 3" diameter, and vertically oriented. The toilet is installed by means of a 3" male or female adopter ring, which is secured to the floor surface. The 3" pipe is attached to the adopter ring. The adopter ring is secured to the floor by means of bolts. A gasket, of sponge rubber or wax, is inserted in the recess in the adapter ring. The toilet is placed in position over the adapter, and is secured to the adapter by bolts. The toilet should be fastened to the floor by other bolts, screws, etc., if holes are provided for such. The main vent for the holding tank, a 1 Y2" ABS plastic vent pipe, is connected to the top surface of the holding tank (at any convenient point) and continues undiminished in size through the roof of the motor coach, and extends 3" above the surface. The opening around the vent should be made watertight by use of appropriate roof jacks or metal flashing.

Following, is the proper method of connecting a shower drain and lavatory drain to the holding tank. The shower pan has a threshold of 4" on all sides except the door, or entrance, which is 3". The floor of the shower pan is sloped from 1/4 to 1/2" per foot toward the drain opening. The drain opening is fitted with a 2 1/2" shower pan drain fitting which connects to a 1 1/2" "P" trap. The "P" trap is in turn connected to a 1 1/2" trap arm. The trap arm should have a slope or grade of 1/4" per foot for its entire length, toward the fixture tee. The trap arm should be no longer than 4'6". The trap arm is in turn connected to a 2" x 2" x 1 1/2" sanitary tee fitting. The lower end of the sanitary tee fitting is connected to a 2" pipe, which is connected to an opening in the top of the holding tank.

The upper end of the sanitary tee fitting is connected to a 2" pipe, which connects to the lower end of the upper (lavatory) sanitary tee.

Now, turn to the proper method of connecting a sink or lavatory to the holding tank. A standard basket strainer is installed in the sink or lavatory drain outlet. The basket strainer is in turn connected to a 1 ½" tailpiece. The tailpiece is inserted into the 1 1/2" "P" trap, which is in turn connected to a 1 1/2" horizontal trap arm. The trap arm has a slope or grade of ¼" per foot of length toward the vent/drain. The opposite end of the trap arm is connected to a 2" x 1 ½" x 1 1/2" sanitary tee. The upper end of the sanitary tee is connected to a continuous vent, extending undiminished in size through the roof of the motor coach. The vent pipe extends 3" above the roof surface. The opening around the vent pipe is made weather tight by means of a vent-type roof jack or metal flashing. The lower end of the sanitary tee (2") is connected to the 2" wet-vented drainpipe. The drainpipe is increased one pipe size below the fixture tee, due to the requirement that it must pass both waste and air. In this case, the shower trap and trap arm are connected into the same drainpipe

Water Distribution System Materials
Water pipes shall be of standard weight brass, galvanized wrought iron, galvanized steel, type K or L copper tubing, or other approved material.

Appropriate fittings shall be used for all changes in direction or size where pipes are joined. The material and design of fittings shall conform to the type of piping used.

Fittings for screw piping shall be standard weight galvanized iron for galvanized iron and steel pipe, and of brass for brass piping. They shall be installed where required for change in direction, reduction in size, or where pipes are joined together.

Fittings for copper tubing shall be cast brass or drawn copper sweat solder pattern or flare type.

Used piping materials shall not be installed. Pipe dope, solder flux, oils, solvents, chemicals, or other substances that are toxic, corrosive, or otherwise detrimental to the water system shall not be used.

Installation of Water Piping
Iron pipe, brass, galvanized iron, plastic or steel pipe and fittings shall be joined with standard pipe threads full engaged in the fittings. Pipe ends shall

be reamed to the full bore of the pipe. Pipe-joint compound shall be insoluble in water and shall be nontoxic.

Copper tubing shall be joined to sweat solder fittings by means of solder and a non-corrosive flux. The surfaces to be soldered shall be thoroughly cleaned without the use of chemicals or self-cleaning fluxes.

A flaring tool shall be used to shape the ends of flared tubing to match the flare of fittings.

Size of Water Supply Piping

Piping shall be sized to provide an adequate quantity of water to each plumbing fixture at a flow rate sufficient to flush and keep the fixture in a clean and sanitary condition without any danger of back-flow or siphonage, except for a fixture specifically approved or listed for other methods of installation or water supply.

Each vehicle equipped with a bathtub or shower and kitchen sink shall be provided with a hot water supply system and water heater.

The size of water supply piping and branch lines shall be not less than sizes shown in the California code at the end of this book. (The California code is obsolete and not included in this work. – Editor)

No galvanized screw piping shall be less than one-half-inch iron pipe size.

Combination compartments limited to 12 square feet or less in floor area may be considered as one fixture.

Sizing for both hot and cold water piping systems shall be computed by the following method: Start at the most remote outlet on any branch of the hot or cold water piping and progressively count towards the water service connection, computing the total number of fixtures supplied along each section of piping. Where branches are joined together, the number of fixtures on each branch shall be totaled so that no fixture is counted twice. Following down the left column of Table in the California Code, a corresponding number of fixtures will be found. The required tubing or pipe size is indicated in the right columns on the same line.

A water heater or food waste disposal unit shall not be counted as a water-using fixture when computing pipe sizes.

Valves installed in the water supply distribution system shall be gate valves except those immediately controlling one fixture supply.

Water Supply Connections

Each vehicle with a water distribution system, which is designed to be connected to an outside source, shall be equipped with a single water supply connection which shall be a three-fourths-inch swivel female hose connection or a one-half-inch or larger pipe connection, sized as required in the Table in the California Code, located as follows: A vehicle designed to be used with motive power, or a recreational vehicle or travel trailer not over 17 feet in length, may have the water supply connection located on either the road or curb side, provided the main drain outlet, natural gas and electrical connections are located on the same side.

The installation of a water supply system shall be made in a manner to preclude the possibility of used, unclean, polluted, or contaminated water mixtures or substances entering any part of the system from any plumbing fixture by reason of siphonage, suction, or any other cause, either during normal use and operation or when any such fixture is flooded or subject to pressure in excess of the operating pressure in the water piping system. No part of the water system shall be connected to any drainage or vent piping.

The outlets of faucets, spouts, and similar devices shall be spaced at least one inch above the flood level of the fixture.

A vacuum breaker shall be installed and maintained in the water supply line on the discharge side of a toilet flush-o-meter valve or manually operated flush valve. Vacuum breakers shall have a minimum clearance of six inches above the flood level of the fixture to the critical level mark.

Toilet flush tanks shall be equipped with an anti-siphon ball cock which shall be installed and maintained with its outlet or critical level mark not less than one inch above the full opening of the overflow pipe. When a back flow prevention device does not bear a critical level marking, the bottom of the vacuum breaker, combination valve, or any such device shall constitute the critical level.

When pressure or gravity-type water supply tanks or reservoirs for storing potable water (except storage-type water heaters or flush tanks) are connected to a water distribution system which has a water supply connection, as provided in this section, the system shall have a spring-loaded check valve or other back-flow prevention device installed in a water supply piping adjacent to the water supply connection. A pressure relief valve shall be required on the outlet side of the check valve, except for systems utilizing gravity-type tanks and where no means for heating water or creating pressure is provided. Pressure relief valves or temperature pressure relief valves on or a part of water heaters may be installed in lieu of the pressure relief valve on the outlet side of the check valve.

A control valve with a minimum internal area equal to the fixture inlet shall be installed in the water supply branch line immediately ahead of each mechanical seal toilet.

Safety Devices

When a check valve or pressure-regulating device is installed between the water supply connection and a storage water heater or closed hot water tank, a pressure relief valve, sized to a BTUH rating equivalent to the BTUH rating of the water heater, or larger, shall be installed.

Pressure relief valves or combination temperature pressure relief valves shall be automatic self-closing type with full-size drain and shall be set to relieve pressure at not more than 125 pounds per square inch (PSI) or at 210 degrees Fahrenheit.

Pressure relief valves shall be installed in the cold water supply pipe between the pressure regulator or the check valve and any water heater or tank, and shall be so located as to be accessible.

Relief valves, if located inside the vehicles, shall be equipped with a full-size metallic drain, which shall extend outside with the end directed downward. No part of the relief drain shall be trapped.

Temperature relief valves or combination temperature pressure relief valves shall be located within three inches of the hottest part of the tank or water heater.

A manually-operated full-way valve or drain plug shall be installed at the lowest point of the water tank or at a point in the water piping system which will permit complete drainage of the tank. The discharge of the valve or drain opening shall extend to the outside of the vehicle.

Water systems incorporating water storage tanks, which may be pressurized by air and to which there is no connection for an outside source of water supplj~7, shall be equipped with an approved air pressure relief valve set to open at 125 psi. The pressure relief valve shall be located at the top of the tank.

Plumbing Fixtures — General Requirements

Plumbing fixtures shall have smooth impervious finishes, free from defects and concealed fouling surfaces, capable of resisting road shock and vibration. Any fixture that may permit back-flow is prohibited.

The waste outlet of all plumbing fixtures, other than toilets, shall be provided with substantial metal strainers that will have an adequate unobstructed waterway.

Fixture tailpieces and continuous waste in exposed or accessible locations shall be minimum No. 20 Brown and Sharpe gauge seamless drawn brass tubing or listed materials. Inaccessible fixture connections shall be constructed according to the requirements for drainage piping.

Each fixture tailpiece, continuous waste, or waste in a recreational vehicle shall be a minimum of one and one-fourth inches for lavatories, sinks or showers having no more than a maximum two-inch drain opening.

Drainage piping shall be provided with inlet fittings for fixture connections, correctly located according to the size and type of fixture to be connected.

Concealed slip joint connections shall be provided with adequately sized unobstructed access panels and shall be accessible for inspection, replacement, or repair.

An approved or listed "Y" or other directional-type branch fitting shall be installed in every tailpiece or continuous waste that receives the discharge from food waste disposal units, dishwashing machines, or other force discharge fixtures or appliances. Dishwasher drains shall not be connected to a sink tailpiece, continuous waste or trap on the discharge side of a food waste disposal unit.

Each toilet shall be equipped with a water-flushing device capable of adequately flushing and cleaning the bowl at each operation of the flushing mechanism.

Toilet flushing devices shall be designed to replace the water seal in the bowl after each operation. Flush valves, flush-o-meter valves and ball cocks shall operate automatically to shut off after each flushing or when the bowl or tank is filled to operating capacity.

Flush tanks shall be fitted with an overflow pipe large enough to prevent flooding at the maximum flow rate of the ball cock. Overflow pipes shall discharge into the toilet through the tank.

Each shower shall be constructed with a finished dam, curb, or threshold at least one inch lower than the sides and back of the receptor. No receptor shall be less than two or more than nine inches in depth when measured from the top of the dam or threshold to the top of the drain. The floor shall slope uniformly to the drain at not less than one-fourth or more than one-half-inch per foot.

Every shower compartment at any point three feet or more above the floor shall be not less than 20 inches in least dimension with a horizontal cross sectional cross sectional area of not less than 400 square inches. The clear standing space of the receptor shall be not less than 12 inches in the least dimension with a floor area of not less then 240 square inches.

The joint around the drain connection, vent, and around the toilet outlet in a combination compartment shall be made watertight by a flange, clamping ring, or other approved means. Hinged shower doors shall open outward.

Shower walls, including showers over bathtubs, shall be constructed of dense nonabsorbent waterproof materials to a height of not less than six feet above the floor.

Shower doors and tub and shower enclosures shall be constructed of materials such as wire glass, laminated safety glass, fiberglass, reinforced plastics, or listed materials.

Each plumbing fixture shall be located and installed in a manner to provide easy access for cleaning, replacement, or repair.

Fixtures shall be set level and in true alignment with adjacent walls. Where practical, piping from fixtures shall extend to nearest wall.

Wall-hung fixtures shall be rigidly attached to walls by metal brackets or supports without any strain being transmitted to the piping connections. Flush tanks shall be securely fastened to toilet or to the wall with adequate-size bolts or screws of brass or other corrosion resistant metal. Metal brackets or supports shall be attached to backing not less in thickness than three-fourths-inch nominal wood or equivalent.

Toilets shall be rigidly bolted to the closet flange, and when screw holes are provided the bowl shall also be solidly fastened to the floor. A gasket or setting compound shall be used to form a watertight seal between the fixture and the drain connection. The exposed joint between the fixture and the floor shall be made watertight. The floor under the toilet and at least six inches around the fixture shall be made impervious to moisture. Floor outlet fixtures shall be rigidly secured to the floor by brass or other corrosion-resistant screws or bolts.

The drain connection for each toilet shall be three inches minimum inside diameter and shall be fitted with an iron, brass, or ABS plastic floor flange adapter ring securely attached to the drain piping.

**As a final reminder,
Technical information in this chapter is decades out of date
and may have been superceded.
Be sure to use the current code.**

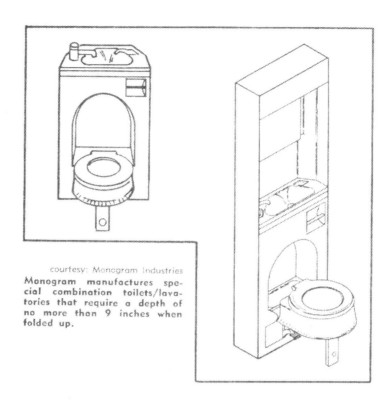

courtesy: Monogram Industries

Monogram manufactures special combination toilets/lavatories that require a depth of no more than 9 inches when folded up.

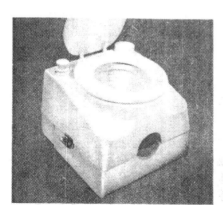

courtesy: Corlon Mfg. Co.

The Corlon Tota-Toilet is portable and can be separated into two units for ease in carrying. The holding tank will accept up to 65 flushes before it must be emptied. Completely portable toilets are one popular solution to sanitation requirements in a bus conversion.

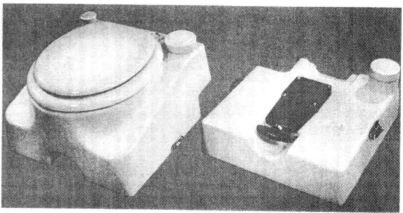

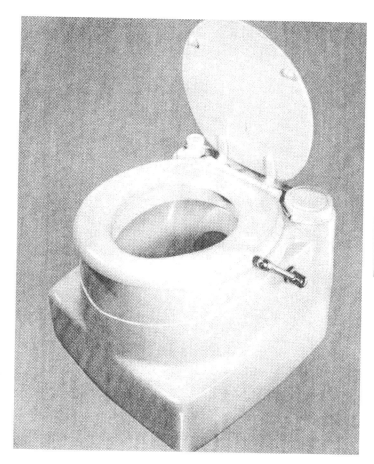

Courtesy: Corlon Mfg. Co.

The Carton, Mini Potti operates off one gallon of water and a packet of chemicals. When the toilet is full it can be emptied using a special outlet provided. It can be emptied at any dumping station or even into a conventional toilet.

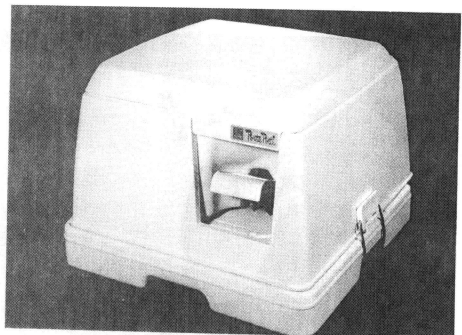

courtesy: Porta Potti

Here is a completely portable toilet whose use you may wish to consider. Note that the compact holding tank separates from the toilet for ease in carrying. The advantage of such a toilet is that no plumbing is required.

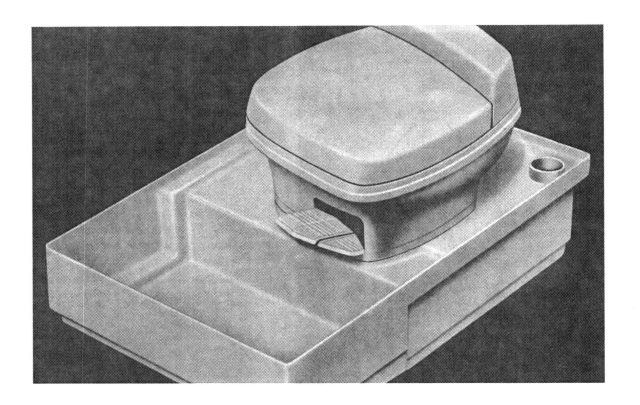

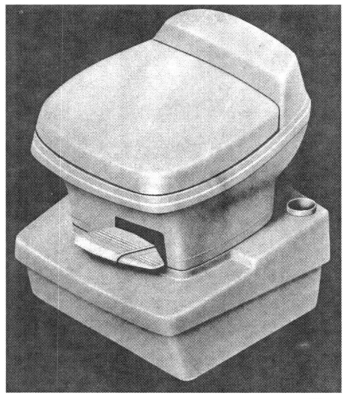

Above is a Thetford combo holding tank and shower pan, combined with an Aqua Magic toilet. The unit is neat and easy to install. A second holding tank is required for all other liquid wastes.

Left is a Thetford Aqua Magic Toilet combined with a Thetford holding tank designed just for the toilet. The unit is neat and simple. It offers the advantage of locating the toilet just about anywhere in the bus conversion without plumbing complications. As with the above unit, a second holding tank is required for all other wastes.

Courtesy: Thetford Corp.

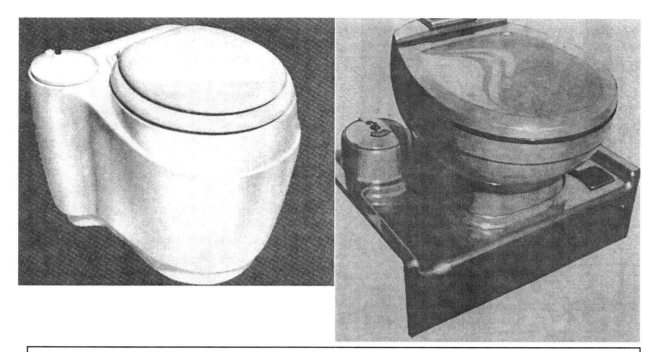

The is the Duomatic sanitation system (top left,) manufactured by Monogram Industries, is a dual system. In one mode, it is the famous Monomatic chemical recirculating toilet. It is completely self contained and can be flushed approximately 160 times before emptying. In the second mode, it is a conventional toilet, hooked up to the park sewer system.

One of the most famous and successful RV toilets is the Monomatic (top right.) The unit is electrical and chemical recirculating. A total of 80 flushes are possible before the toilet must be emptied. This is accomplished by use of a Full Way valve that leads either to a termination plug or to a holding tank. The toilet is not portable.

Courtesy: Monogram Industries, Inc.

Below is a schematic rendering of one of Thetford's holding tamnks. The capacity of this one is 13 gallons.

Courtesy: Thetford Corp.

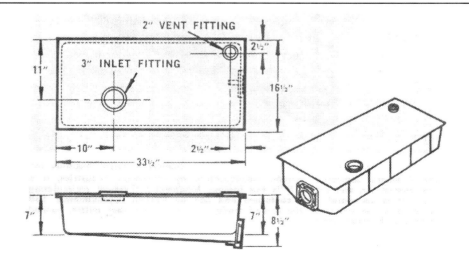

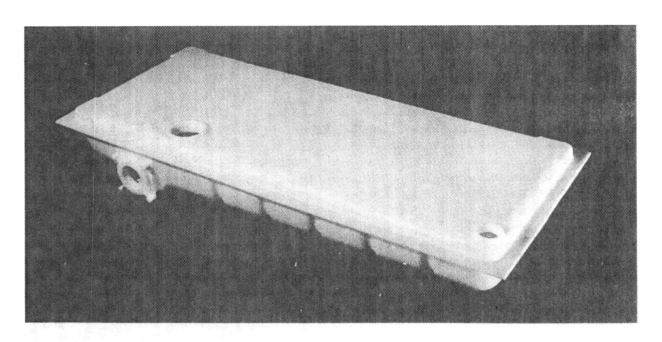

Thetford manufactures many different holding tanks whose capacity and configurations vary. All include a 3″ inlet, a 3″ outlet and a 2½″ vent fitting.

Waste Plumbing Drawings

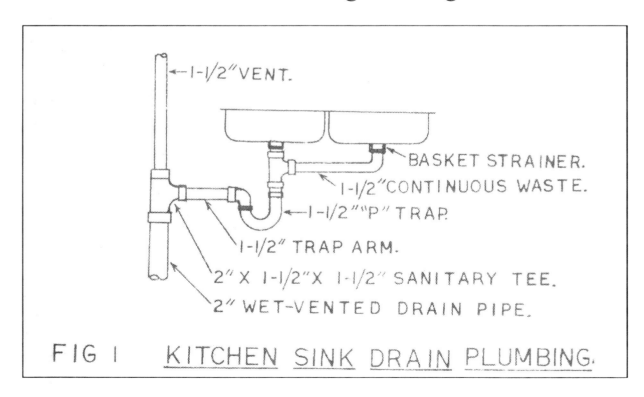

1-1/2″ VENT.

BASKET STRAINER.

1-1/2″ CONTINUOUS WASTE.

1-1/2″ "P" TRAP.

1-1/2″ TRAP ARM.

2″ X 1-1/2″ X 1-1/2″ SANITARY TEE.

2″ WET-VENTED DRAIN PIPE.

FIG I   KITCHEN SINK DRAIN PLUMBING.

Waste Plumbing Drawings, continued

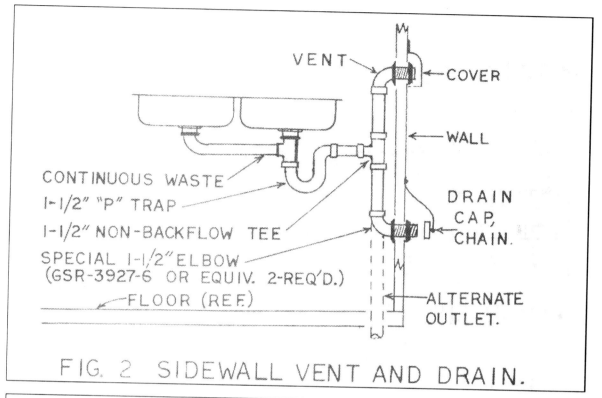

VENT — COVER

WALL

CONTINUOUS WASTE

1-1/2" "P" TRAP

1-1/2" NON-BACKFLOW TEE

SPECIAL 1-1/2" ELBOW
(GSR-3927-6 OR EQUIV. 2-REQ'D.)

FLOOR (REF.)

DRAIN CAP, CHAIN.

ALTERNATE OUTLET.

FIG. 2 SIDEWALL VENT AND DRAIN.

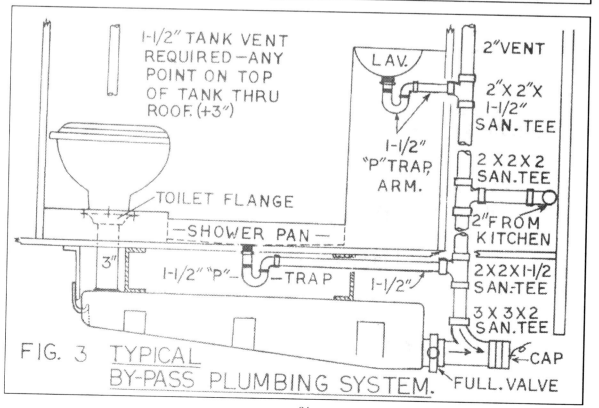

1-1/2" TANK VENT
REQUIRED—ANY
POINT ON TOP
OF TANK THRU
ROOF. (+3")

LAV.

2" VENT

2" X 2" X 1-1/2" SAN. TEE

2 X 2 X 2 SAN. TEE

1-1/2" "P" TRAP, ARM.

2" FROM KITCHEN

TOILET FLANGE

SHOWER PAN

3"

1-1/2" "P" TRAP

1-1/2"

2 X 2 X 1-1/2 SAN. TEE

3 X 3 X 2 SAN. TEE

CAP

FULL. VALVE

FIG. 3 TYPICAL BY-PASS PLUMBING SYSTEM.

Waste Plumbing Drawings, continued

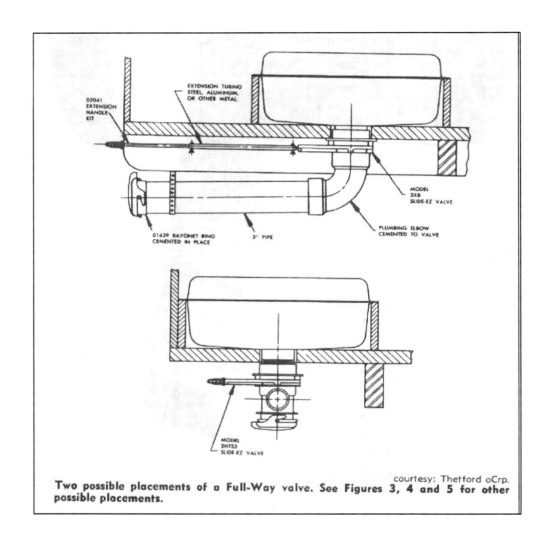

Two possible placements of a Full-Way valve. See Figures 3, 4 and 5 for other possible placements.

courtesy: Thetford oCrp.

Waste Plumbing Drawings, continued

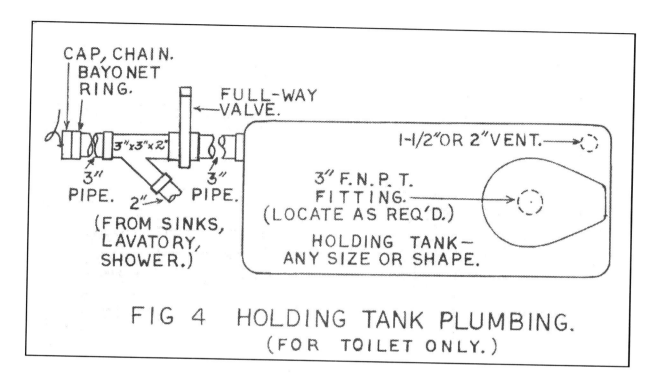

CAP, CHAIN.
BAYONET
RING.

FULL-WAY
VALVE.

3"x3"x2"

3"
PIPE.

2"

3"
PIPE.

(FROM SINKS,
LAVATORY,
SHOWER.)

1-1/2" OR 2" VENT.

3" F.N.P.T.
FITTING.
(LOCATE AS REQ'D.)

HOLDING TANK-
ANY SIZE OR SHAPE.

FIG 4 HOLDING TANK PLUMBING.
(FOR TOILET ONLY.)

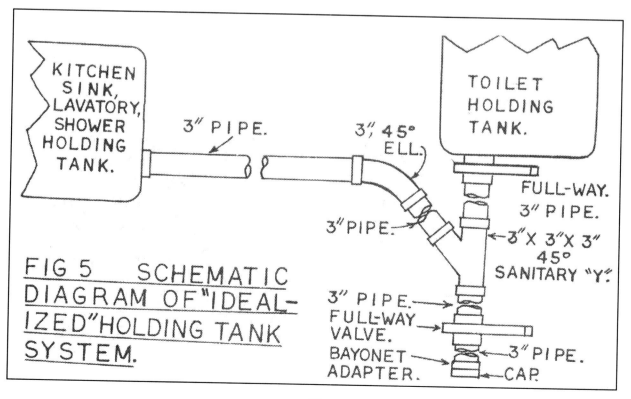

KITCHEN
SINK,
LAVATORY,
SHOWER
HOLDING
TANK.

3" PIPE.

3", 45°
ELL.

3" PIPE.

TOILET
HOLDING
TANK.

FULL-WAY.
3" PIPE.

3" X 3" X 3"
45°
SANITARY "Y".

3" PIPE.
FULL-WAY
VALVE.

BAYONET
ADAPTER.

3" PIPE.

CAP.

FIG 5 SCHEMATIC
DIAGRAM OF "IDEAL-
IZED" HOLDING TANK
SYSTEM.

Waste Plumbing Drawings, continued

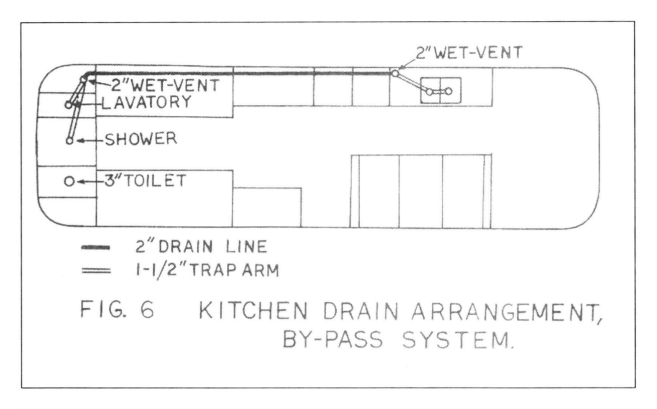

FIG. 6   KITCHEN DRAIN ARRANGEMENT,
BY-PASS SYSTEM.

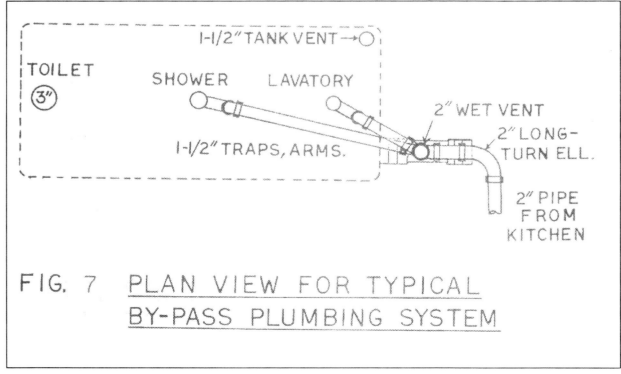

FIG. 7   PLAN VIEW FOR TYPICAL
BY-PASS PLUMBING SYSTEM

Water Supply Drawings (typical)

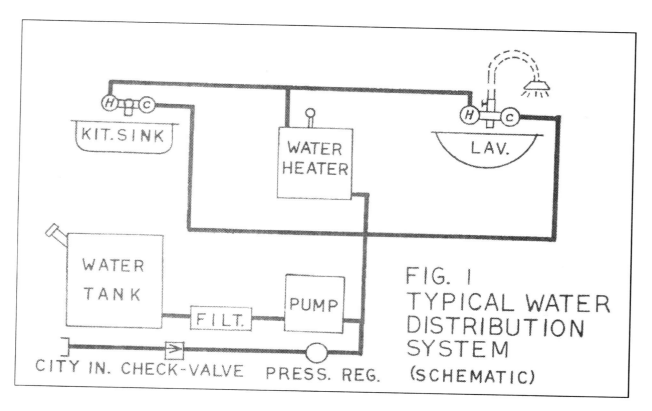

FIG. 1
TYPICAL WATER
DISTRIBUTION
SYSTEM
(SCHEMATIC)

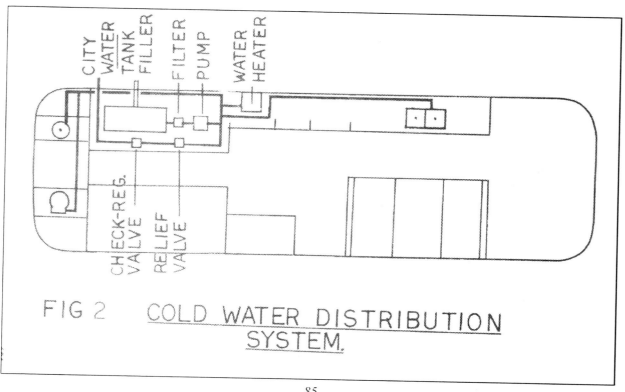

FIG 2   COLD WATER DISTRIBUTION
SYSTEM.

Water Supply Drawings (typical)

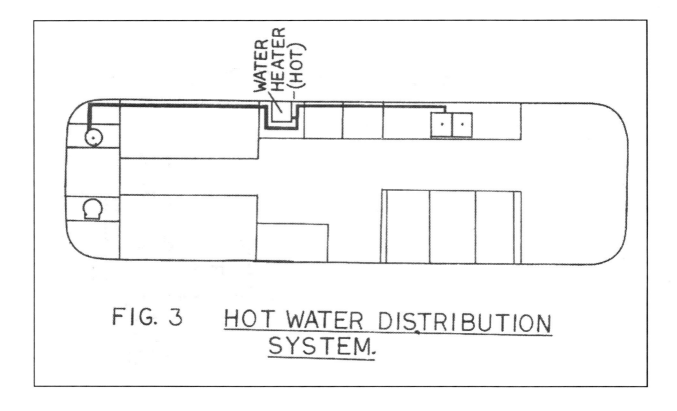

FIG. 3   HOT WATER DISTRIBUTION SYSTEM.

Illustrated here is a modern 12-volt "on demand" type water pump for use in RVs and bus conversions. When you turn on a faucet the pump recognizes a drop in water pressure and automatically activates. When demand ceases (you turn off the valve) the pump pressurizes the system and shuts itself off, going into standby mode until it is needed again.

The pump moves water as opposed to older systems that pumped air into the water storage tank.

The disadvantage of the air pressure system was that the storage tank had to be heavy duty to withstand the air pressure. Additionally you needed to carry an air pump or air storage tank.

Refer to Figure 1 on Page 85 for placement of the pump. Note that it serves both the hot and cold water systems.

Courtesy of ITT Industries.

http://www.flojet.com/

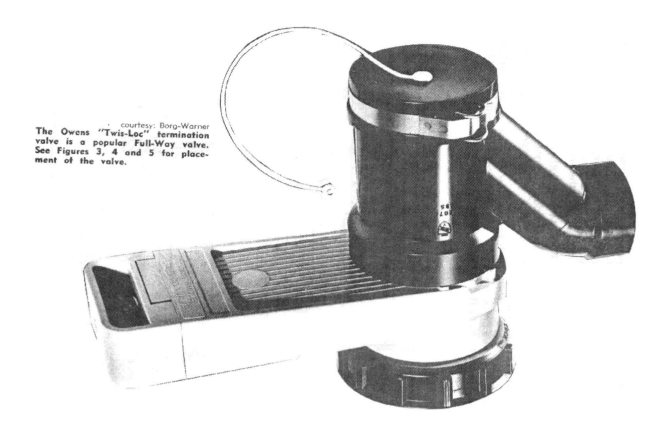

courtesy: Borg-Warner

The Owens "Twis-Loc" termination valve is a popular Full-Way valve. See Figures 3, 4 and 5 for placement of the valve.

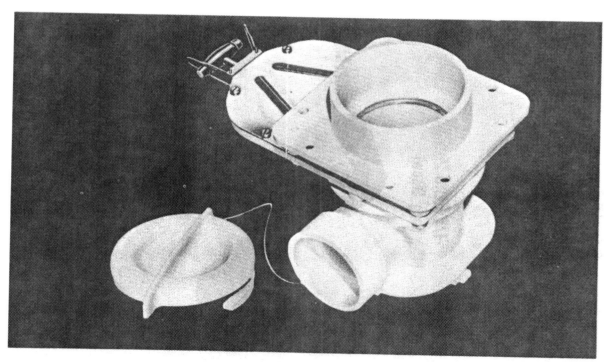

courtesy: Thetford Corp.

Thetford "Slide-EZ Valve" is one of a number of Full-Way valves on the market. The valve is used to evacuate your holding tank and effectively seal it at other times.

87

Note: Black pipe fittings, shown in the following pages, should be used for **waste plumbing only**. While many converters use copper pipe for water supply, some use white plastic water system pipe. See your plumbing or hardware store for the correct pipe if using plastic.

Plastic Pipe Fittings by
R&G Sloane Manufacturing Company.

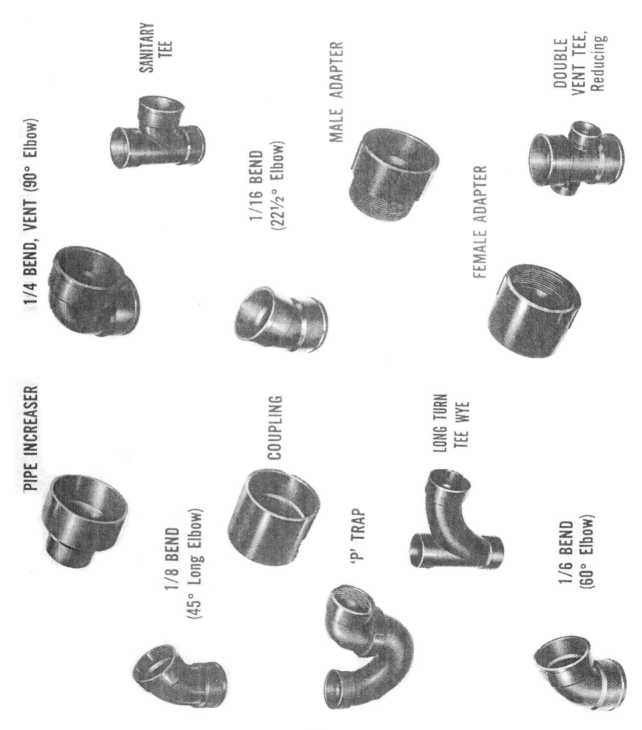

SANITARY TEE

1/4 BEND, VENT (90° Elbow)

1/16 BEND (22½° Elbow)

MALE ADAPTER

FEMALE ADAPTER

DOUBLE VENT TEE, Reducing

PIPE INCREASER

1/8 BEND (45° Long Elbow)

COUPLING

'P' TRAP

LONG TURN TEE WYE

1/6 BEND (60° Elbow)

Note: Black pipe fittings, shown in the following pages, should be used for **waste plumbing only**.
While many converters use copper pipe for water supply, some use white plastic water system pipe.
See your plumbing or hardware store for the correct pipe if using plastic.

Plastic Pipe Fittings by
R&G Sloane Manufacturing Company.

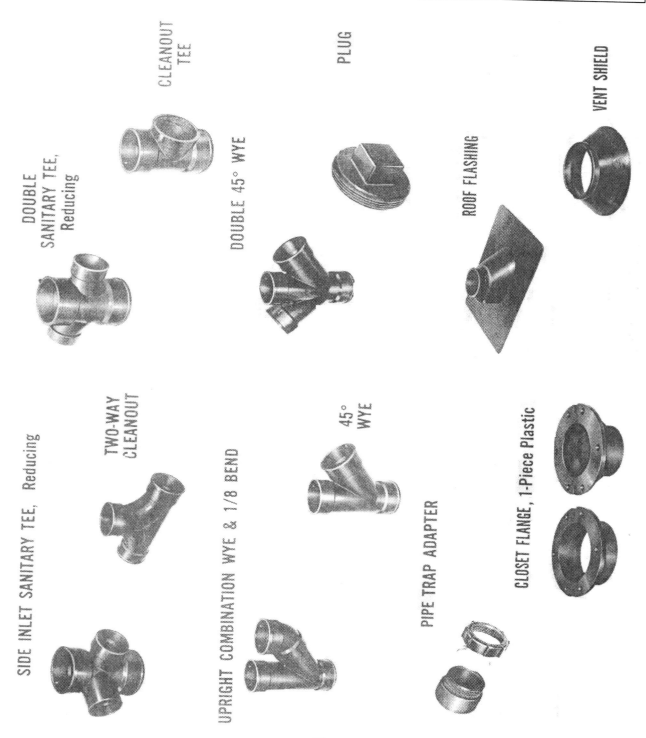

DOUBLE SANITARY TEE, Reducing

CLEANOUT TEE

DOUBLE 45° WYE

PLUG

ROOF FLASHING

VENT SHIELD

SIDE INLET SANITARY TEE, Reducing

TWO-WAY CLEANOUT

UPRIGHT COMBINATION WYE & 1/8 BEND

45° WYE

PIPE TRAP ADAPTER

CLOSET FLANGE, 1-Piece Plastic

Do's and Don'ts When Installing Plastic Pipe

Note to the 2002 edition: These specifications were accurate at the date of original publication. However, advances in plastic pipe and glues have changed. Consult the product documentation for current data.

1. Use only standardized and approved DWV pipe fittings and solvent cement. Look for the marks CS27O, CS272, NSF and NSF DWV on all products to be sure of the quality.

2. Cut pipe square, using a hand saw and miter box, a mechanical cut off saw, or a plastic pipe cutter which does not raise a burr on the end of the pipe.

3. Don't use a standard wheel cutter, It will raise a flare on the end of the pipe. The flare will scrape the cement from the joint and create a leak.

4. Remove all burrs from the end of the pipe with a file or knife. If all the burrs are not removed they may scrape lines in the cement and create leaks.

5. Clean and dry the pipe and fitting socket of all dirt, moisture, and grease. Use a clean dry rag.

6. Use only solvent cements carrying the ASTM specification number and/or the NSF seal of approval. Use only ABS cement for ABS pipe and fittings and PVC cement for PVC products. Unapproved or unknown brands of cement may contain substances that can damage the pipe & fittings.

7. Don't use thinner to dilute the solvent cement. Discard the cement if it thickens very much in the can. Keeping the cement can closed as much as possible while working will help to prevent thickening.

8. Dry fit the pipe into the fitting socket. It should enter at least ½ of the socket depth, and should at least snug up at the socket bottom in ABS parts. For PVC parts, a little looseness at the socket bottom can be tolerated.

9. For ABS components, first coat the inside of the fitting socket, then coat the outside of the pipe. Flow the cement on with a full brush. Assemble parts immediately with a quarter turn to spread the cement evenly.

10. For Type I PVC parts (PVC 1120 or 1220), degloss flue pipe and fitting socket with cleaner — MEK, MIBK or acetone, or lightly sand the surfaces before applying cement. Coat the pipe first, then the socket, then a second coat on the pipe Again,

assemble immediately, with a quarter turn. Allow freshly made joints to set a few minutes before moving or applying any force to them.

11. Use only approved thread tape or thread lubricant specifically intended for making up threaded joints.

12. Don't use conventional pipe thread compounds, putty, linseed oil base products or unknown mixtures. They can cause cracking of the parts.

13. Threaded connections should be made up one turn past hand tight, using a strap wrench. Over tightening may damage the parts.

14. Don't pull or force pipe into line when assembling. This stresses both pipe and fittings and can lead to tutu. trouble.

15. Allow for thermal expansion in all installations by allowing freedom for the pipe to move with temperature changes. Leave the pipe free to move longitudinally at changes in directions and on long straight runs, but support it at four foot maximum intervals.

16. Refer to IAMPO installation standards IS 5-66 and IS 9-68 for full information on thermal expansion.

17. Use threaded transition fittings when connecting to copper systems. Caulked joints or other approved fittings may be used in connecting plastic to cast iron.

18. Use caution when heating lead for caulked joints. Heat it to just above the melting point. A good rule to follow is to heat the lead to wiping temperature.

19. Use common salt or calcium chloride solutions for antifreeze, where necessary. If preferred. ethylene glycol antifreeze may be used.

20. Don't use alcohol antifreeze in any part of the plastic DWV system.

Courtesy of : R&G Sloan Manufacturing Company

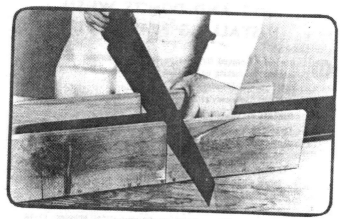

Pipe must be cut as square as possible. Use a hand saw and mitre box or mechanical saw. A diagonal cut reduces the bonding area in the most effective part of the joint.

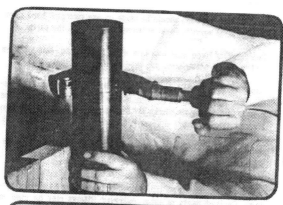

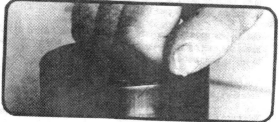

Plastic tubing cutters may also be used for cutting plastic pipe. However, some produce a raised head at the end of the pipe. This must be removed as it will wipe the cement away when pipe is inserted into fitting.

Remove all burrs from both the inside and outside of the pipe with a knife, file or reamer. Burrs can scrape the channels and create hangups on the walls.

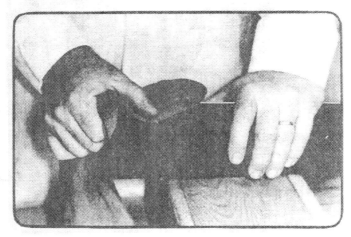

Remove dirt, grease and moisture from the pipe fitting. A thorough wipe with a clean dry cloth is usually sufficient. Moisture can retard cure and dirt or grease can prevent adhesion.

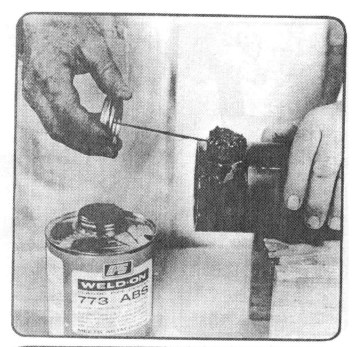

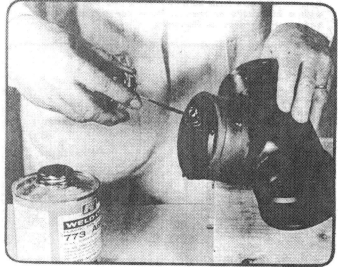

Apply a medium layer of cement to the fitting socket. Avoid puddling. Apply a full even layer of cement to the pipe, equal in depth to the socket. Flow the cement on with the applicator . . . do not brush it on thinly. The cement layers on the pipe and fittings must both be without voids and sufficient to fill any gap in the joint.

Assemble the pipe and fittings without delay. The cement must be wet. Use sufficient force to ensure that the pipe bottoms in the fitting socket. Twist the pipe if possible when inserting. Hold the pipe together for about a minute to ensure proper seating. There is a tendency for the pipes to separate at first because of the taper.

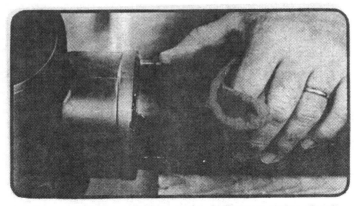

After assembly, a joint will have a ring or bead of cement completely around the juncture of the pipe and fitting. If voids in this ring are present, sufficient cement was not applied and the joint may de defective.

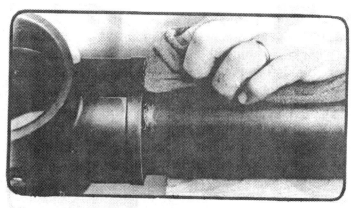

Using a rag, remove all the excess cement from the pipe and fitting. Otherwise, the pipe will be needlessly softened. Avoid disturbing or moving the joint, however.

Handle newly assembled joints carefully until they are dry. The length of time for drying varies from six hours to four days, depending on the temperature, humidity and size of pipe. The manufacturer will supply you with a chart to determine the time in your particular case.

Note to the 2004 edition: The drying time was accurate at the date of original publication. However, advances in plastic pipe glues have changed drying time requirements. Consult the documentation on the product to verify current drying times.

16. Motor Coach Electrical Systems

Important note to the 2004 edition:

**Many of the suggestions and directions in this chapter
are based on electrical codes of the 1970's
While these guidelines are sound, certain aspects of the codes on which they are based
may have been superceded with more recent specifications.
Be sure to compare this information with current RV building codes.**

TYPICAL POWER REQUIREMENTS FOR VARIOUS APPLIANCES

Appliance	Watts (@ 120 Volts)	Amperes
Table lamp, 100-watt bulb	100	.83
Table fan	75	.60
Television set	300	2.50
Table radio	150	1.25
Coffee percolator	600	5.00
Automatic toaster	1100	9.00
Blender	250	2.10
Deep fryer	1300	11.00
Roaster	1300	11.00
Mixer	150	1.25
Hand iron	1000	8.30
Electric refrigerator (motor)	250	2.10
Garbage disposer	600	5.00
Electric water heater	1000	8.30
Air conditioner	1300*	11.00
Electric room heater	1000-up	8.30-up

*While running; usually requires approximately twice this amount
for starting.

TABLE II

CURRENT CARRYING CAPACITIES FOR VARIOUS WIRE SIZES

Size, AWG	Current-carrying capacity, amperes
14	15
12	20
10	30
8	40
6	55
4	70
3	80
2	95
1	110

Note: Sizes smaller than AWG 14 (larger number indicates smaller
wire size) should not be used for wiring motorcoaches.

Designing the 120-volt Electrical System

Lighting Requirements:

Ample lighting fixtures must be provided to ensure adequate illumination throughout the entire motor coach. Generally, lighting fixtures should be installed in the bathroom, bedroom, kitchen, dining, and lounge areas.

The lighting circuit should have a minimum circuit capacity of 3 watts per square foot of floor area, based upon the outside dimensions of the vehicle. Thus, for a motor coach 26 feet in length, by eight feet in width, the minimum circuit capacity would be:

$$26 \times 8 \times 3 = 624 \text{ watts}$$

Converting watts into amperes at 120 volts, we obtain

$$\frac{624}{120} = 5.2 \text{ Amperes}$$

Figure 1

This means that the lighting circuit must be capable of providing at least 5.2 amperes for illumination throughout the coach. This is the minimum circuit capacity. However, the lighting circuit may be capable of providing greater capacity if desired. Also, this does not mean that the lighting circuit must draw 624 watts, but that a minimum of 624 watts must be available for lighting. In actuality, the lighting circuit may draw considerable less or considerably more than 624 watts, depending upon the number and wattage ratings of the righting fixtures installed. The actual wattage, when all lights are ON, can be determined by merely adding all the wattage ratings of both the incandescent and the fluorescent fixtures.

Motor coaches having a combined total of not more than six general appliance and lighting outlets may have either

(1) One branch circuit, 15 amperes, to supply these outlets, provided the total rating of fixed appliances connected to this circuit does not exceed five amperes or 600 watts; or

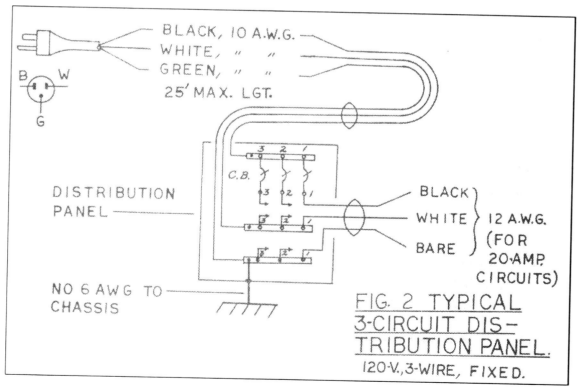

FIG. 2 TYPICAL 3-CIRCUIT DISTRIBUTION PANEL. 120-V., 3-WIRE, FIXED.

Fig. 2 shows how a power cord is wired. There is no receptacle attached to the exterior of the coach to receive the power cord. The power cord is hard-wired directly to the electrical panel.

(2) One, branch circuit, 20 amperes, to supply these outlets, provided the total rating of the fixed appliances connected to this circuit does not exceed nine amperes or 1,000 watts.

When vehicles are wired in accordance with (1) or (2) above, no electrical heating or cooking appliances may be installed.

As we determined above, 5.2 amperes at 120 volts (624 watts) are required for the lighting circuit capacity. However, if we design the lighting circuit for 15 amperes capacity (1800 watts), and require 624 watts for the lighting circuit, then we have a surplus capacity for other appliances. According to (1) above, we may use the lighting circuit to provide up to 600 watts of power (Or five amperes) to operate other appliances. Likewise, according to (2) above, if we design the lighting circuit for 20

amperes capacity (2400) watts) and require 624 watts for the lighting circuit, then we also have a surplus capacity for other appliances. In this case we may use the lighting circuit to provide up to 1,000 watts of power (or nine amperes) to operate other appliances. Therefore, the lighting circuit may be utilized to operate both the lights and certain small appliances. This is sometimes referred to as a general purpose lighting circuit. It is often installed in the simpler systems. For the 15 ampere circuit, No. 14 AWG copper wire should be used, with a 15 ampere circuit breaker. For the 20 ampere circuit, No. 12 AWG copper wire would be used, with a 20 ampere circuit breaker.

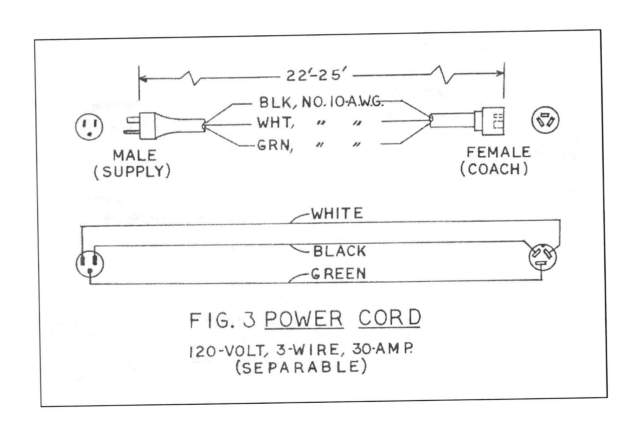

FIG. 3 POWER CORD
120-VOLT, 3-WIRE, 30-AMP.
(SEPARABLE)

Fig. 3 shows how an extension cord may be wired in order to connect from the power supply to the plug at the end of the fixed cord. All standard 3-wire power cords are normally wired in this manner. A much better method would be to buy a simple adapter available at any RV store or park for just a few bucks and use a standard heavy-duty cord.

A typical wiring diagram for a single
circuit 15 or 20 ampere general purpose
lighting circuit is shown in Figure 4.

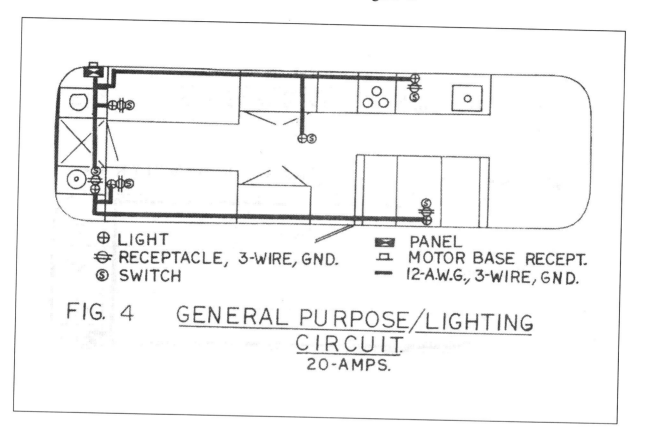

⊕ LIGHT   ▭ PANEL
⊖ RECEPTACLE, 3-WIRE, GND.   ᴅ MOTOR BASE RECEPT.
Ⓢ SWITCH   ▬ 12-A.W.G., 3-WIRE, GND.

FIG. 4   GENERAL PURPOSE/LIGHTING
                        CIRCUIT
                        20-AMPS.

Your entire 110 volt
system must be
grounded and every
outlet should have a
grounding lug.

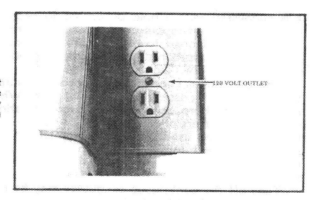

120 VOLT OUTLET

120-volt Portable Appliance Circuit

Receptacles in the kitchen and dining areas of motor homes should be connected to a separate portable appliance circuit, of 20 amperes capacity. A 20-ampere capacity circuit has a wattage capacity of 2400 watts. No combination of appliances exceeding 2400 watts should be used on this circuit at any one time. The wire should be AWG 12, and a 20-ampere circuit breaker should be installed. All receptacles should be 3-prong grounding type.

Be sure to use GFCI (Ground Fault Circuit Interrupter) outlets, especially in the kitchen and bath. This safety device is designed for use in wet areas as an added protection against electrocution.

The portable appliance circuit is required to supply power to operate portable appliances such as a coffee percolator (600 watts), automatic toaster (1100 watts), blender (250 watts), deep fryer (1300 watts), roaster (1300 watts) mixer (150 watts), hand iron (1000 watts) and other portable electric

appliances which may require relatively high amperage. Connecting these high-wattage appliances to a general-purpose circuit may cause an overload.

These portable appliances are normally used in the kitchen and dining areas. Therefore, outlets in these areas may be connected to this separate portable appliance circuit.

It is desirable to install a duplex outlet above the kitchen base cabinets, on each side of the kitchen sink(s), provided there is at least 12 inches of counter-top on each side. Also, on outlet should be provided adjacent to the dining table, to accommodate toaster, percolator, etc. Another outlet should be provided adjacent to the refrigerator or freestanding gas range provided electrical circuits are contained in the units.

A typical wiring diagram for a separate portable appliance circuit is shown in Figure 5.

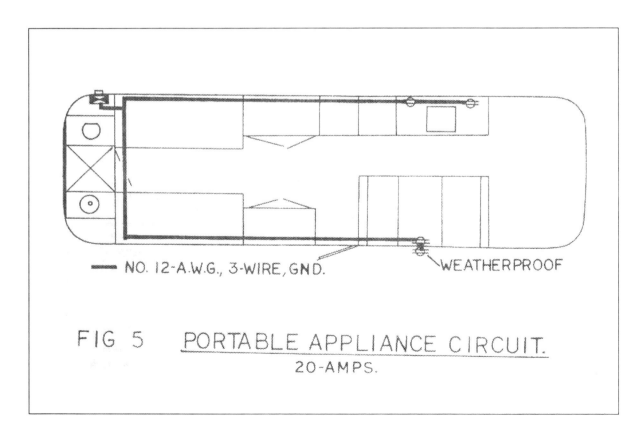

— NO. 12-A.W.G., 3-WIRE, GND.   WEATHERPROOF

FIG 5   PORTABLE APPLIANCE CIRCUIT.
20-AMPS.

120-volt Fixed Appliance Circuit

Certain appliances installed in a motor coach are often permanently connected into the electrical system. Therefore, they may be permanently located and wired directly into the system, or may be connected by means of a suitable receptacle and plug.

Such appliances as an electric water heater (1000 watts), an electric room heater (when permanently installed) (1000 watts and up), an air conditioner (1300 watts operating, 2500 watts starting), or an electric hotplate (1600 watts) are not usually required to be moved from one location to another. Therefore it may be desirable to permanently install them on a separate electrical circuit in the motor coach. Obviously, the outlets for these appliances should be located as close to the appliance as practical. Usually they are located in remote areas where they are not likely to be accessible for other uses.

The current-carrying capacity (amperes) of the fixed appliance circuit will depend upon the number and wattage of the units connected to the circuit. (Refer to Table], Typical Power Requirements For Various Appliances). Power requirements for fixed appliances can be very high. For this reason, it is often advisable to use another source of energy for operating these appliances where possible. (Substitution of gas-fired appliances for electrical appliances. There are certain functions that may be operated more efficiently by gas than by electricity. These should be thoroughly investigated before installing the appliances).

A wiring diagram for a separate fixed appliance circuit is shown in Figure 6.

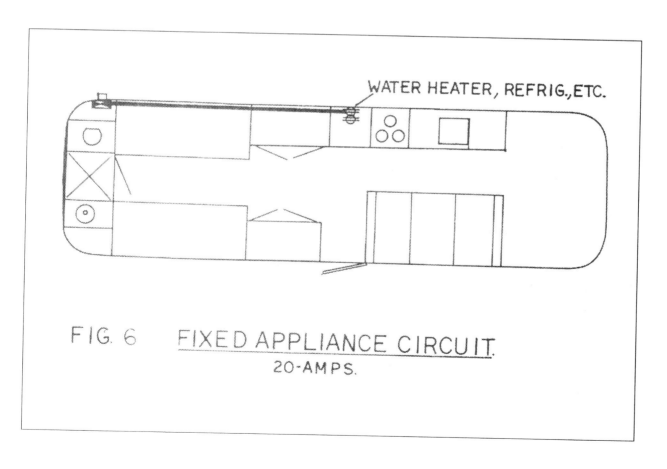

WATER HEATER, REFRIG.,ETC.

FIG. 6   FIXED APPLIANCE CIRCUIT.
20-AMPS.

120-volt Air Conditioner Circuit:

Air conditioners usually require from 12 to 15 amperes of current to operate, and approximately twice that amount for starting. Therefore, it is necessary to install a separate circuit for operation of the air conditioner.

As the air conditioner requires so much electrical power to operate, it is common to operate the air conditioner(s) from a separate power source, such as an on-board motor generator set. A motor-generator rated at 2500 watts should be the minimum for operation of the air conditioner, especially if other electrical loads will be connected to the motor-generator also. The starting current for the air conditioner can usually be supplied by the motor-generator set if the other loads are not too great. The starting current requirement is for a very short period of time, until the air conditioner comes up to normal operating speed. At this time, the current requirements stabilize at from 12 to 15 amperes per air conditioner. This represents from 1440 to 1800 watts respectively. Therefore considering a minimum lighting circuit capacity of

the original 624 watts for our hypothetical 26-foot motor coach, a 2500-watt motor-generator would be about the minimum size recommended. If two such air conditioners are installed, then a 4000 to 5000 watt motor-generator is recommended.

However, the air conditioner may be operated from the external power source also. Normally, the external power source and cable assembly are rated at a nominal 30 amperes capacity. (3600 watts continuous duty). Such a system could easily provide power for starting and operating a single air conditioner unless other high-wattage appliances were operated at the same time.

Whether the air conditioner is operated from the external power source or from an on-board motor-generator set, the Circuit would be the same. The difference would be in the manner of energizing the main distribution panel. (To be discussed in more detail under motor-generator sets).

A typical wiring diagram for a single or dual air conditioner circuit is shown in Figure 7.

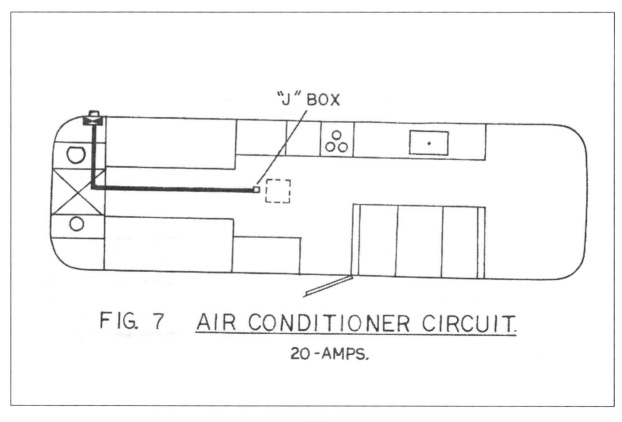

FIG. 7   AIR CONDITIONER CIRCUIT.
20-AMPS.

120-Volt electrical System
Converter Circuit

A converter is a device, which changes 120 volts alternating current (AC) to 12-volts direct current (DC). It may only be operated when a source of 120-volts AC is connected.

It is necessary to make provisions for operating lights and certain other appliances and accessories whether 120-volts AC is available or not.

In order to accomplish this, 12-volt DC lights, appliances, and accessories are often installed in motor homes. In addition, extra batteries may be installed to provide the power to operate these lights, accessories, and appliances. However, there must be means provided for recharging the batteries and operating these devices when the motor coach is connected to 120-volts AC.

When the motor coach is connected to 120-volts AC, the converter changes the 120-volts AC into 12-volts DC to operate all the 12-volt DC lights, appliances, and accessories. In addition, most converters also charge the batteries when connected to 120-volts AC.

When the motor coach is not connected to 120-volts AC, either from an external source or from an one-board motor-generator set, the batteries are used to provide the required power to operate these 12-volt lights, appliances, and accessories. Thus, all of the 12-volt DC lights, appliances, and accessories operate regardless of whether 120-volts AC is connected or not. This system provides freedom to operate independently of 120-volt power sources.

batteries either from a motor-driven generator or alternator, an on-board

motor-generator set or connecting the motor coach to an external 120-volt AC source. The amount of time which a motor coach may be operated on batteries depends upon the number and type of lights, appliances, and accessories installed and operated, conservation of battery power by turning off unnecessary lights, appliances, and accessories, and of course on the capacity of the battery system itself.

Installation of a converter circuit in a motor coach may be as simple or as complex as desired. There are various types of automatic sensing circuits available to enable recharging the batteries at a specified point interconnecting the converter with the vehicle battery; "cross-tying" the auxiliary batteries with the vehicle battery for starting purposes; cross-tying the auxiliary batteries with the vehicle charging circuit to recharge the auxiliary batteries, etc. These devices are very convenient and are somewhat automatic in operation, but are considered beyond the scope of this book in detail.

The converter circuit, permitting the use of all 12-volt DC lights, appliances, and accessories, is becoming more popular with motor coach owners. There are certain appliances, however, which are more practical to operate from 120-volt AC sources, such as air conditioners, heaters, and cooking units. This makes a combination 120-volt AC/12-volt DC system most practical.

There are many appliances and accessories designed to operate from 12-volts DC. Some of these are lights, water pump, fans, blowers, stereo hi-fi systems, refrigerators, coffee makers, television sets, etc.

However, operation of these devices when the motor coach is not connected to an external 120-volt AC source or an on-board motor-generator set, or operation of the vehicle motor, may rapidly discharge the batteries. Therefore, provisions must be made to recharge the

courtesy: Onan Electric Co.
Illustrated here is a 2500 watt, 120 volt power generator specifically designed for motor homes. The unit gives you full self-containment regardless of the availability of electric power. Although equipment such as this is built for quiet operation, method of installation affects noise greatly. Be sure to use heavy duty rubber grommets in mounting and to provide generous insulation against sound.

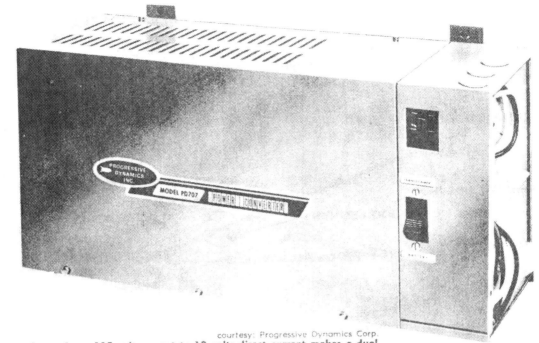

courtesy: Progressive Dynamics Corp.

A converter that reduces 115 volt current to 12 volts direct current makes a dual electrical system unnecessary since all current delivered to appliances is 12 volt, regardless of whether it comes from a battery or park utility. The unit pictured above also recharges the recreational vehicle battery when it is operating in the 115 volt mode.

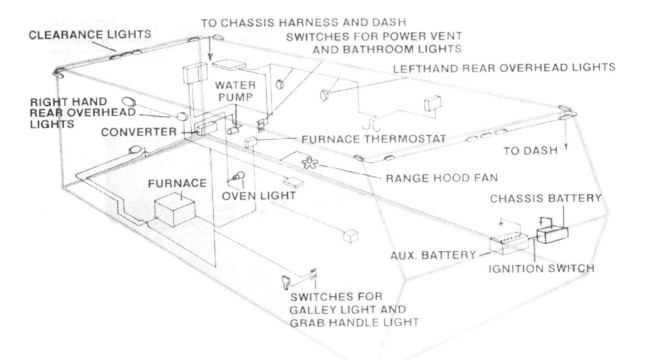

GENERIC DIAGRAM OF 12 VOLT WIRING CIRCUITS

12-volt Direct Current Electrical System Lighting Circuit

As in the case of designing the 120-volt AC lighting system, there should be ample 12-volt lighting fixtures to ensure adequate illumination throughout the entire motor coach. Generally, a 12-volt direct-current lighting fixture should be installed in the bathroom, bedroom, kitchen, dining, and lounge areas.

There are no minimum lighting capacity requirements for 12-volt DC lighting systems. Considering that these lights will often be operated from batteries, it is usually desirable to be as conservative as possible when installing 12-volt DC lighting fixtures, both in the number of fixtures installed and the amount of current required by each.

12-volt DC lighting circuits may be installed in addition to the 120-volt AC lighting circuits, or the 120-volt AC lighting circuits may be deleted if the 12-volt DC circuits and a converter are installed.

The design and installation of the 12-volt DC circuit is identical whether used with a converter system or directly connected to the 12-volt batteries. Each circuit in the 12-volt DC distribution system should be limited to 20 amperes. This can be determined by reference to the nameplate or descriptive literature on the particular fixture to be installed. Each circuit should consist of at least No. 10 AWG copper wire for the continuous conductors. Taps may be as recommended by the fixture manufacturer or as provided on the fixture. Each circuit should be protected by one separate 20 ampere circuit breaker. A master or main circuit breaker, of approximately 40-ampere rating should protect the entire system.

When installing a 12-volt DC circuit, the chassis of the motor coach is commonly used as the ground conductor. It is important that the batteries or the converter be securely grounded to the chassis, preferably by means of a battery ground strap for batteries, or at least No. 8 AWG wire for the converter circuit. Make sure that good electrical connections are made between the fixture and the chassis, if using the chassis as the ground conductor. It is suggested that a hole be drilled to accommodate a No. 8 sheet metal or self-tapping screw, and the area around the hole be thoroughly cleaned to bright metal by sanding or using steel wool. Install an appropriate size lug to the ground wire, and install with a No. 8 screw. Tighten screw securely.

The continuous conductor should be protected by means of a grommet where it passes through metal parts. Where the conductor bends around sharp corners, additional insulation should be provided. Several layers of electrical tape or other insulating jacketing material may be used. The conductor should be secured as required to prevent movement, which may cause abrasion of the insulation, and to prevent mechanical strain from being placed on the conductor.

Taps off the continuous conductor may be made by removing the insulation (do not cut wire) approximately 1 inch long where the tap is to be made. Cut the tap wire to length plus approximately 1 1/2 inches. Strip the insulation from the end of the tap wire, and wrap the end of the tap wire tightly around the bare continuous conductor. Solder may be applied if desired. Wrap the entire connection with several layers of insulating plastic tape. Secure the continuous conductor and the tap wire in place to prevent movement or mechanical strain. Protect the wiring from possible physical damage.

17. Liquefied Petroleum Gas (LPG)

Liquefied Petroleum Gas (LPG) is used extensively in motor coaches for heating, cooking, hot water heating and refrigeration. An LPG system can enable a motor coach to operate completely independently of all outside power.

Most motor coaches use LPG for at least some of the above mentioned functions. Many use LPG for all those functions.

Liquefied Petroleum Gas (LPG) is a liquid when compressed, and gaseous when not compressed. LPG weighs approximately 4 pounds per gallon in liquid state. LPG is forced into a pressure-type cylinder under high pressure in a liquid form. An air space is provided above the liquid level, which is filled with gas. The outlet from the pressure is under high pressure, and the pressure must be reduced to safely operate appliances. A pressure regulator is installed at the outlet of the tank to reduce the maximum pressure in the main and distribution lines to approximately 6 to 8 ounces per square inch. Gas at this pressure is then fed to the various appliances.

The size of the gas piping used throughout the motor coach depends upon the maximum total BTU input rating of the appliances. For total BTU inputs of 38,000 BTUH or less, 3/8" copper tubing may be used. For total inputs up to 88,000 BTUH, 1/2" pipe or 5/8" copper tubing may be used. Motor coaches seldom exceed 88,000 BTUH total input.

LPG tanks must be securely installed on the vehicle. They should be installed in such a manner as to support a static load of 10 times their filled weight. Tanks should be installed such that the lowest part of the LPG tank is above the level of the lower edge of the horizontal portions of the rear axle of the vehicle on which they are mounted, when the vehicle is fully loaded.

LPG containers may be obtained with fuel quantity gauges built-in, or gauges may be purchased separately and installed instead of the 10 percent valve. For permanently mounted tanks, a fuel quantity gauge is almost a necessity. For removable tanks, a gauge is a definite convenience. LPG tanks have the tare weight of the tank stamped on the plate affixed to the tank. This is the empty weight of the tank. Also, the full weight of the tank is indicated on the plate. In the absence of a gauge, the tank may be weighed to determine the amount of fuel in the tank. A scale for this purpose is available through camper, trailer, and motor home supply stores. However, the cost of a scale may well equal the cost of a simple outage gauge. It is impractical to remove a large, permanently mounted tank for filling.

Propane tanks should be installed in a location, which will ensure that the tank is not subjected to physical damage. If mounted at the rear of the motor coach, it should be adequately protected by a sturdy bumper. Tanks may be mounted underneath the vehicle, between the frame rails if desired. Remote filling kits are available which permit extensions to be attached to the outside of the coach. A fill tube and an "outage" tube are provided, along with the necessary check valves and fittings.

LPG leak detectors are also available. One popular type provides instantaneous "push button" leak check of the entire gas distribution system. Another type detects the presence of gas in the interior of the motor coach.

The piping or tubing used in the LPG distribution system should be in accordance with the code. Piping or tubing should be installed in such a manner that it will not be subject to damage. The tubing should be routed adjacent to structure where possible, and be secured in place at frequent intervals using suitable clamps. Only Type K or Type L copper tubing should be used. Brass flare type fittings should be used throughout.

After installation of the filled LPG tanks, a leak check should be made of all fittings in the system. Use soapy water to make the leak test. Apply soapy water liberally with a small brush to every fitting while observing that no air bubbles are formed. (Air bubbles indicate gas leaks). Tighten all fittings securely.

Warning:
DO NOT use lighted matches to detect gas leaks. Fire or explosion may result.

Protect tubing at points where it may possibly be damaged due to chafing or rubbing. Use appropriate-sized grommets where tubing passes through metal parts. Do not rely upon tubing fittings and connections for the total support of tubing.

Filling LPG containers not equipped with Quick-Fill device: Disconnect "pigtail" connector spud and nut from POL valve. Attach filler nozzle to POL valve. Open "10 percent" valve. Open filler valve and POL valve. Allow container to fill until liquid begins coming out of the "10 percent" valve. Shut off POL valve and filler valve. Shut "10 percent" valve. Disconnect filler nozzle from POL valve and reinstall tank as necessary.

Filling LPG containers equipped with Quick-Fill device: Remove cap from Quick-Fill connection. Attach filler nozzle. Open filler nozzle valve. Open the 10 percent valve. When liquid begins coming out of the 10 percent valve, close filler nozzle valve, and close 10 percent valve.

LPG tanks may be mounted in special gas tight compartments recessed into the side of the motor coach. The compartment should be gas tight to the inside of the coach. The door of the compartment should be of the same size as the overall dimensions of the compartment. The door should be vented by means of louvers located at the top of the door; the louvers should comprise at least two percent of the front area of the door. The compartment should be vented through the floor of the comportment to the outside of the coach.

The tanks should be securely installed within the compartment. Tanks should be mounted in their normal orientation, and so arranged as to be easily removed and reinstated. If more than one tank is installed, a sensing device should be installed to automatically switch over to the full tank when one tank is empty. It should be possible to remove the empty tank for refilling without interrupting the flow of gas to the coach.

An approved pressure regulator should be installed between the LPG tank(s) and the main distribution line. The regulator may be installed in any position. Special "pig-tails" with spuds and nuts installed are available for connecting the LPG tank valve to the regulator.

The regulator should be connected to the main supply line through a flexible hose, terminating in a gas tight bulkhead fitting through the compartment wall.

The door of the compartment should be fitted with simple latches that do not require tools or a key to open.

The LPG compartment and/or tank(s) should not be located near a LPG appliance that is vented through the wall. Also, the tanks should not be located near hot engine or exhaust parts.

LPG tanks may be installed beneath the vehicle, and attached directly to the chassis frame or to the floor. In such cases, the lowest part of the LPG tank, valves, or fitting, should be above the lowest horizontal portion of the rear axle of the vehicle on which it is mounted. The tank should be securely attached to the vehicle frame or floor, and be capable of withstanding a vertical force of approximately ten times the filled weight of the tank without becoming dislodged from its mounting.

LPG tanks should **always** be installed in the position for which they were designed. A tank, which is designed for vertical installation, should not be installed horizontally, or at an angle. Like wise, a tank designed for horizontal mounting should never be installed in a vertical position. Some tanks designed for horizontal mounting may have the quick-fill valve, the POL valve, and the 10% valve located either at the top or the bottom of the tank. Some manufacturers are now identifying the TOP of the tank, and the tank should always be installed in its proper orientation. In the event the tank is not labeled TOP (some older tanks were not) the manufacturer's nameplate should always be normal (not inverted).

Tanks should never be modified in any way. Do not weld additional supports, mounts, etc., to the tanks, as the tanks have been pressure tested at the factory. To weld onto a tank may weaken the tank and cause failure. Do not modify any portion of the valves, guard, or mounting hardware. The guard is designed to protect the valves in case the tank is accidentally dropping on a flat surface.

Modern LPG tanks are fitted with a so-called "10%" or "outage" valve. This valve senses the level of the liquid in the tank, and signals the operator to cease filling the tank. Liquid is vented out the "10%" valve when the maximum permissible liquid level is reached. DO NOT overfill an LPG tank.

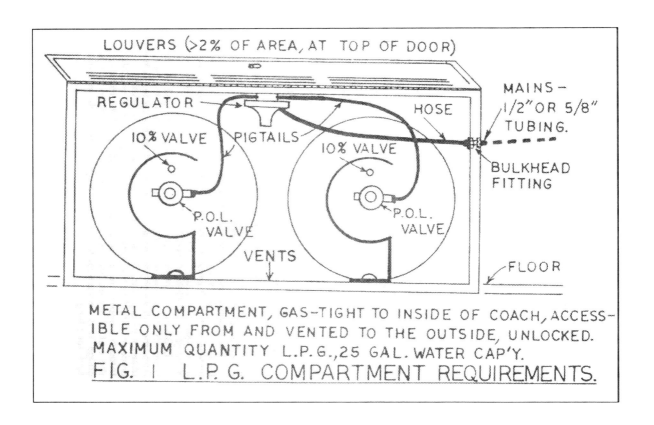

LOUVERS (>2% OF AREA, AT TOP OF DOOR)

REGULATOR

HOSE

MAINS - 1/2" OR 5/8" TUBING.

10% VALVE

PIGTAILS

10% VALVE

BULKHEAD FITTING

P.O.L. VALVE

P.O.L. VALVE

VENTS

FLOOR

METAL COMPARTMENT, GAS-TIGHT TO INSIDE OF COACH, ACCESSIBLE ONLY FROM AND VENTED TO THE OUTSIDE, UNLOCKED. MAXIMUM QUANTITY L.P.G., 25 GAL. WATER CAP'Y.

FIG. 1 L.P.G. COMPARTMENT REQUIREMENTS.

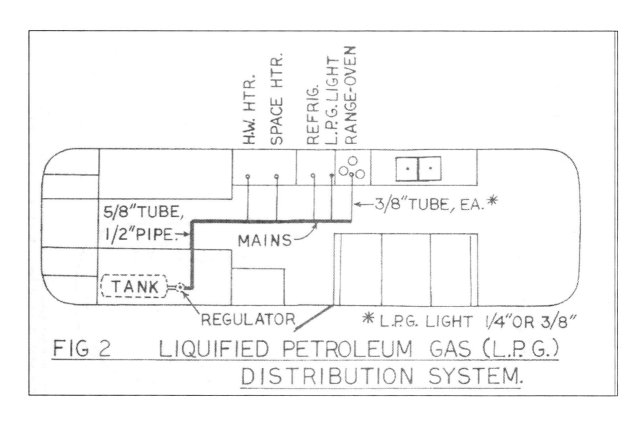

HW. HTR.
SPACE HTR.
REFRIG.
L.P.G. LIGHT
RANGE-OVEN

3/8" TUBE, EA. *

5/8" TUBE, 1/2" PIPE.

MAINS

TANK

REGULATOR

* L.P.G. LIGHT 1/4" OR 3/8"

FIG 2   LIQUIFIED PETROLEUM GAS (L.P.G.) DISTRIBUTION SYSTEM.

Fuel lines should be fastened securely under floor every 2 to 3 feet.

Fuel lines must be protected by rubber grommets where they pass thru the floor.

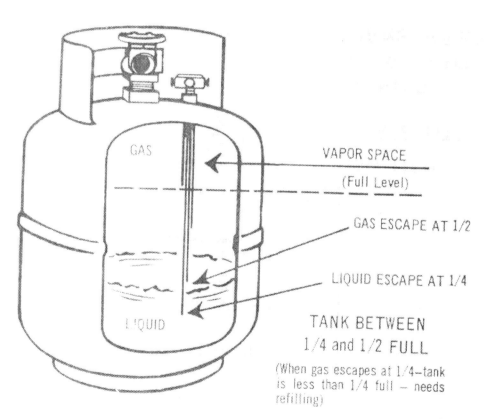

GAS

VAPOR SPACE

(Full Level)

GAS ESCAPE AT 1/2

LIQUID ESCAPE AT 1/4

TANK BETWEEN
1/4 and 1/2 FULL

(When gas escapes at 1/4—tank is less than 1/4 full — needs refilling)

LIQUID

Courtesy: Marsh Mfg. Co.

This liquid level gauge replaces the conventional 10% valve and enables you to determine the level of liquid in tank by a series of dip tubes.

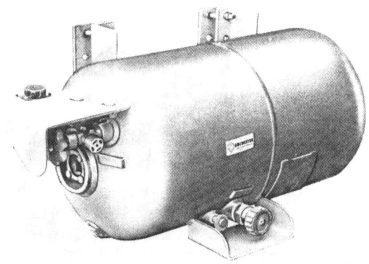

Some LPG tanks are equipped with a Quick Fill device that permits filling the tank without disconnecting hookup to the interior of your bus. This tank is equipped with a special window that permits you to check the amount of gas still in the tank. It is located below the POL valve on the side. Ten percent valve is next to the Quick Fill device.

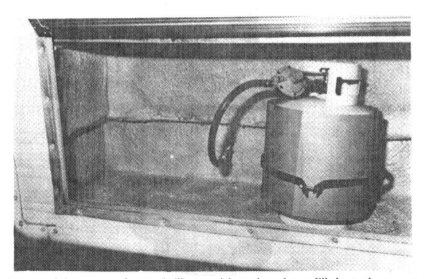

A one tank butane supply area is illustrated here. In order to fill the tank, remove the hose and pressure regulator and attach hose from filling tank. Pressure in the filling tank is far greater so gas flows to yours. Note construction of compartment for tank, which must be air tight with respect to the inside of your conversion and vented with respect to the outside.

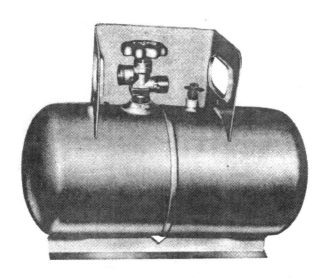

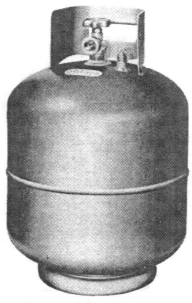

Tanks are made either for vertical or horizontal mounting. Never install a tank in a position different from what it was built for. On both of these tanks you can see the POL valve and the ten percent valve. The POL valve must be twisted shut when disconnecting the pigtail and connecting the fill hose. The lower of the two projections from the POL valve is a safety valve which breaks if pressure in the tank is too great.

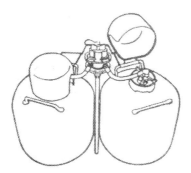

Use double cylinder installation instead of a single cylinder. It's safer and you'll enjoy better service.

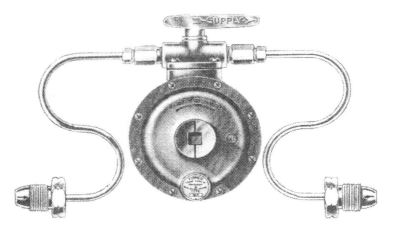

This double system gas regulator automatically switches over to the second tank when the contents of the first is exhausted. Handle at top indicates which tank is in service. Once you are working off the second tank you should fill the first.

One advantage of the double tank gas regulator is that you can disconnect and fill one tank while the other is operational – no disruption of gas service! (Editor)

18. Safety, Maintenance and Operation

Fortunately, a motor coach is one of the safest vehicles on the road. Buses are designed to safely transport the full load of passengers that they will seat. A typical bus may weigh 16,000 pounds when empty, and have a maximum gross vehicle weight (GVW) rating of 26,000 pounds. The difference between the maximum rated GVW and the empty weight is called the "payload". The maximum GVW is usually stamped on a placard in the driver's compartment.

In the above case, with a maximum GVW of 26,000 pounds, and an empty weight of 16,000 pounds, we have a payload capacity of 10,000 pounds. When this bus is converted into a motor coach, it may have a maximum gross weight of perhaps 20,000 pounds. Thus, we have a safety factor of 6,000 pounds before we reach the maximum GVW of the vehicle. Many recreational vehicle (truck-mounted campers, some trailers and factory made motor homes) have gross weights approaching or in some cases exceeding their maximum GVW ratings. Some of these vehicles are dangerously overloaded!

The maximum GVW rating of a vehicle is the maximum gross weight including vehicle and payload that the chassis is designed to safely carry. When operated with the maximum GVW ratings, there is sufficient safety factor built into the vehicle to accommodate normal road shock, vibration, and other stresses imposed upon the chassis during normal operation.

Exceeding the maximum rated GVW of a vehicle may cause premature failure of the chassis components, as well as create safety hazards. Most manufacturers' warranties are voided if the maximum rated GVW is exceeded. Fortunately, it is not likely that a bus will exceed its rated maximum GVW when converted into a motor coach. In all likelihood, it will have ample safety margin.

Buses are inherently stable. This is due to their weight, massive frames, heavy suspension components, tires, and weight distribution. They are little affected by strong cross winds or by passing trucks. The conversion of a bus into a motor coach has negligible effect upon the weight distribution of the vehicle, and does not affect its stability.

Buses usually provide much better visibility when driving than do automobiles, due to their greater height. When driving a bus, the road can be seen for a considerable distance ahead. The driver can see over automobiles and small trucks, and has a much better picture of the traffic situation ahead. Likewise, he has considerably more time to react to a developing traffic situation.

In addition to providing the driver with a better view of the road, buses are also more easily seen by other drivers. Automobile drivers who may be inclined to take a chance when passing, while meeting another automobile, are not inclined to take such chances when meeting a bus. There's something to be said about sheer size.

In case of a collision with another vehicle, there is less likelihood of serious injury to passengers in a bus than in an automobile. Recent tests have been made to determine the degree of protection offered passengers in buses when the bus was struck in the side by a standard automobile traveling at highway speed. The bus was stopped. The bus did not overturn, and suffered only superficial damage. (The frame was not damaged). Mannequins inside the bus, simulating passengers, were tossed about inside the bus. However, had they been secured with seat belts, it is doubtful whether serious injury would have resulted to the passengers. The automobile was a total loss, and any passengers who may have been riding in the automobile would have been fatally injured.

Insurance: Always carry sufficient insurance on your coach to protect others in the event of an accident. While the exact amounts of insurance may vary, amounts of $100,000/$300,000 are suggested. Higher amounts of insurance are available, and the cost is relatively small.

Insurance is becoming increasingly more difficult to obtain, especially for home conversions. They are considered "high risk." You can usually forget anything beyond liability insurance.

Safety Equipment

Every motor coach should be equipped with the following safety items:

1. A serviceable fire extinguisher approved by the

Fire Underwriters Laboratories and the U.S. Department of Transportation. Place the fire extinguisher in an easily accessible location, and make sure all persons are familiar with the proper use of the fire extinguisher.

1. A set of approved U.S. Department of Transportation flares, or equivalent, to be used in case of a break-down on the highway. A minimum of three flares should be included.

1. A large wooden block or other object which may be used as a wheel chock to prevent rolling of the coach in case the brake system is inoperative, or the coach should become disabled on a grade. The chock may be used for other purposes if desired.

1. Large rear-view mirrors located on either side of the coach for maximum rearward visibility. Wide-angle mirrors are also recommended in order to enable the driver to see a wide area behind or beside the coach. Smaller automobiles are often difficult to see when beside the coach. This is particularly helpful when changing lanes.

1. Adequate hydraulic jack capable of lifting the rear dual wheels of the coach. Also, adequate tools and equipment to permit changing a wheel if necessary.

1. A serviceable flashlight with fresh batteries.

1. An approved first aid kit.

Tires: Most buses use dual wheels on the rear. Since the bus is usually lightly loaded when converted into a motor coach as compared to carrying a full load of passengers, the rear tires are not required to carry the full rated loads.

Anyone who has driven an empty bus knows how rough they can ride. This is particularly true of the conventional and the transit type buses, and to a lesser degree for the interstate type. It is common practice to reduce the air pressure in the rear tires of a motor coach to soften the ride. For example, a tire that should normally be inflated to 70 pounds pressure may be reduced to 55 pounds in most cases. Reducing the tire pressure significantly below 55 pounds may cause excessive heat build-up and cause premature tire failure.

Recapped tires are often used on the dual rear

wheels of motor coaches. These recapped tires are entirely satisfactory for use on the dual rear wheels. Most school buses, interstate trucks and trailers, etc., use recapped tires on the rear duals with excellent results. Tires may be recapped twice if desired. The savings effected through use of recapped tires on the rear duals are considerable.

Recapped tires should never be used on the front wheels of a bus or motor coach. Always use first-run (not recapped or retread) tires on the front of a motor coach. Front tires should have a minimum of one-sixteenth of an inch of visible tread depth at the center of the tread.

Inspect all tires on your motor coach frequently. As a fast check, a hammer may be used to tap the tires periodically when stopped. (Truck drivers normally use this method). However, it is recommended that an accurate truck tire gauge be used before departing on a long trip, and at intervals throughout the trip. Do not depend upon service station gauges for accuracy!

Brakes: Before driving your motor coach, always check the brakes. If the coach is equipped with hydraulic or vacuum-assisted hydraulic brakes, depress the pedal firmly. The pedal should not go to the floor, nor require "pumping" to obtain a firm pedal. When clear, put the coach in motion (slowly) and apply the brakes. Do not drive the coach if the brakes are faulty.

If the coach is equipped with air brakes, (not safety spring brake equipped), start the engine and observe that the air pressure gauge increases steadily up to 100 to 120 pounds. The gauge should stabilize in this range. If the coach is equipped with a low air pressure warning buzzer, it should sound until approximately 60 PSI is reached, then stop. There should be no indication of air escaping from the system. Depress the brake pedal. The pedal should be firm. The air pressure indicated on the pressure gauge should drop slightly (approximately 2 to 4 psi) and stabilize immediately. Hold the pedal depressed and determine that the air pressure does not leak down rapidly. (No more than 2 psi per minute). Put the coach in motion (slowly) and apply the brakes. If the coach is equipped with air brakes and safety spring brakes, start the engine and observe that the air pressure gauge increases steadily up to 100 to 120 pounds. If equipped with a low air pressure warning horn or light, the warning device should be activated until the pressure reaches approximately 60 psi. The gauge should stabilize between 100 to 120 PSI. Depress the brake pedal. The pedal should be firm. The pressure gauge should drop slightly and stabilize. There should be no rapid drop in the air pressure. Without releasing the spring brakes, shift into a low gear and release the clutch slightly to determine whether the spring brakes are ON. Release the spring brakes. Put the coach in motion (slowly) and apply the brakes. Braking action should be normal.

The air pressure tanks installed in the air brake system should be drained frequently. Petcocks are installed at the lowest point on the tanks. Open the petcock after each trip, or more often if needed, and allow the air and water to drain out. If the coach is equipped with spring brakes and an auxiliary reserve tank, drain the reserve tank also. Close the petcocks securely after draining.

Belts: Most buses use belts to drive the fan, generator or alternator, air compressor and water pump. These belts should be inspected for wear, breaks, separation of plies, cracking, etc., at frequent intervals. Replace any defective belt as soon as possible.

Many coaches use matched pairs of belts to drive some of the accessories. These belts must be replaced in pairs. They are matched for length, and thus carry equal loads. Replacing only one belt will cause one belt to carry considerably more of the load (due to unmatched lengths) and cause early belt failure.

Belts used on trucks and buses are usually much larger and stronger than those used on automobiles. They are industrial types, usually reinforced with nylon, steel cable, or other material. Ordinary automotive belts usually cannot withstand the severe loads imposed on them when used on a bus.

Tighten belts until approximately 3/4" to 1" of free play is obtained midway between the sheaves. Do not over tighten, as this will cause early belt failure, or possibly bearing failure. Too loose belts will cause belts to overheat and early belt failure. Applying belt dressing to the belt while operating can quiet squeaking belts. Always be sure to carry an extra set of belts for your coach, as they may be difficult to obtain in certain areas, or may cause undue delays. The author has had the sad experience of having to replace a pair of matched belts on a trip, necessitating hiring a taxi ($15.00) to go to a distant town, and paying $25.00 for a pair of matched belts — when he had a new set of matched belts at home!

Radiator Hoses: Inspect all radiator and heater hoses periodically just as you would on your automobile. Replace any hoses that have become brittle, cracked, excessively bulged, or cut. It is especially important to check the hoses before installing antifreeze solution, to prevent loss of the antifreeze in case of a hose failure. Tighten all hose clamps. Insure that the lower radiator hose cannot collapse under suction. Check the operation of the thermostat by running the engine a few minutes and observing that the temperature gauge stabilizes at the proper point. (This should coincide with the temperature rating of the thermostat, between 160 and 190 degrees). For winter operation, a 180-degree thermostat is recommended. Do not operate the coach without a thermostat installed, as this will not permit the engine to come up to normal temperature, or will not allow the engine to stabilize at the proper temperature. Too rapid heating or cooling of an engine can be harmful.

Check the radiator cap for sealing and pressure operation. Service stations normally have pressure cap test fixtures to test the opening pressure of the radiator cop. Replace the cap if it opens at too low pressure, as indicated on the cap.

Inspect the radiator coolant to determine that there is no excessive accumulation of rust in the cooling system. If the water is rusty, or there are other signs of overheating, the radiator should be removed and cleaned. Cooling efficiency is often critical in some types of buses, especially the rear-engine transit types. When the cooling system is in good condition, cooling should not be a problem. However, on very hot days, and when climbing long continuous grades, some tendency to overheat may be encountered. It is often a help to turn on the heater(s) inside the coach to help cool the engine. Often, a 10-degree difference can be realized by turning on the heaters. This could mean the difference between satisfactory operation and overheating.

Crankcase Oil: Check the level of the engine oil each day the coach is in service and monitor the oil pressure frequently while driving. If the oil pressure should drop to an abnormally low value while driving, stop the engine and investigate the cause of the problem. Often it may be low oil level, or excessive engine temperature. Oil pressure drops when the engine reaches a critical temperature.

Most buses require the use of SAE 30, 40 or 50 oil under normal conditions. For continuous operation in hot weather, SAE 50 may be used. **In any event, use the rating recommended by the engine manufacturer.**

Engine oil should be changed at regular intervals, either based upon miles driven or hours of operation. Oil filters should also be changed at regular intervals. Dirty, diluted, or contaminated oil can cause excessive wear to vital engine parts.

Oil performs two vital functions in an engine: lubrication and cooling. Normally, engine oil should operate at approximately 20 degrees hotter than the engine coolant. Oil tends to break down rapidly above 250 degrees F. For this reason, it is recommended that an oil cooler be installed on bus engines. The life expectancy of the engine will be increased, and the maximum permissible RPM's of the engine may be increased slightly when an engine oil cooler is installed. (Approximately 100 RPM increase).

Electrical system: The distributor and spark plugs used in bus engines are usually identical to those used in automobile engines. Points should be inspected periodically to determine that there are no burrs or pits on the surface of the points, and the point gap is within the specified range. Replace burned or pitted contact points. The condenser is normally replaced at the same time. The new points should be installed, the gap adjusted, and, if a dwell meter is available, the points should be checked to determine that the proper degree of dwell is obtained. The timing should be adjusted by means of a timing light. Worn sparkplugs should be replaced. Brittle, cracked, or otherwise deteriorated ignition cables should be replaced.

Carburetor Air Filter: Air filters filter out dust, dirt, etc., from the air entering the carburetor. Air filters may become clogged after only a few hours of operation under extremely dusty conditions. Under normal conditions, air filters should be serviced (oil-bath types) or replaced (dry filter types) as recommended by the engine manufacturer. Clogged air filters tend to prevent free engine breathing, resulting in a richer mixture, and reducing operating economy.

Lights, Turn Indicators, Markers, Tail and Stop Lights, Etc.: Inspect the operation of all lights on your motor coach at frequent intervals, and replace any bulbs, lamps, fuses, switches, etc., as required

to maintain all devices in proper working order. Disable red alternately flashing school bus lights.

A motor coach represents a considerable investment in money and labor. Usually, your family will be traveling with you in your motor coach. Remember that you have a great deal of responsibility in your hands — the safety of your family, yourself, your motor coach, other vehicles and passengers. It is imperative therefore that you exercise extreme care in the operation of your motor coach. Carelessness on your part could have serious consequences. The amount of damage that can be done with a motor coach is tremendous.

Always drive your motor coach defensively. Keep your vehicle under complete control at all times. Do not speed. Do not tailgate. Be extra careful when passing or changing lanes, and allow ample distance and clearance when passing. Do not consume alcoholic beverages while driving or before driving. Do not change drivers while the coach is in motion. Keep your coach in good mechanical condition, and do not operate your coach with known or suspected faulty equipment.

Always be alert when driving your motor coach. If you should become drowsy or tired, either change drivers or stop and rest.

When, you observe a string of vehicles following your coach on narrow roads, pull off at the first opportunity and allow other vehicles to pass safely. Many states have a "5 vehicle rule". If you are holding up more than 5 vehicles, you can be cited.

Always shift into a lower gear when descending a long grade. A motor coach is heavy, and will gather speed on long downgrades. Shift into a lower gear at the start of the downgrade to save wear on the braking system. Do not wait until the coach has gained excessive speed and then try to downshift. In many cases it is very difficult to downshift when the coach is traveling at a high rate of speed.

Do not use your brakes constantly on long downgrades. Brakes tend to heat up rapidly, and fading may result. Always keep your coach under complete control to the extent that you could completely stop the coach should the need arise.

Most motor coach owners soon learn that traveling in their motor coach to and from an event can be as much fun as the event itself. In your motor coach, you are free to converse, move about, relax, enjoy refreshments, take a nap, stop when and where you please, etc. You arrive at your destination relaxed and refreshed. After the event, you look forward to the drive home. Again, you arrive home rested, relaxed and refreshed, instead of tired and weary from a long hard drive. You are more alert, less accident-prone.

You'll soon discover that with a motor coach, getting there and back is as much fun as being there!

Good Luck, and may you have
many years of happy motor coaching!

Although not part of this chapter, rather than leave most of a page blank, I offer these additional photos.

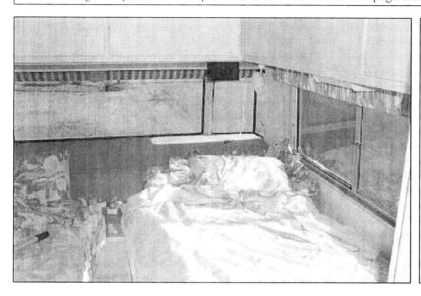

Most converters opt for a traditional double or queen bed in the master bedroom at the rear of the coach.

This usually results in a "tight fit" and making the bed is difficult. Additionally, the use of overhead cabinets is limited because they would be in the walk area or over the bed where access would be difficult.

With twin beds you have a center aisle and making the bed is much easier and overhead cabinets are easily accessible. Additionally, convertible lounges would make for a comfortable day room when not used for sleeping.

Well designed rear lounge. The lounge has a full entertainment system and the sofa makes into a bed.

19. Tachometers, Governors, Transmissions and Rear Axles

It is highly recommended that buses be equipped with accurate tachometers, or governors. In my opinion, a tachometer is preferable to a governor, providing the bus is operated by persons who will not exceed the maximum allowable RPM. A tachometer will tell you when to shift either upward or downward, yet you may exceed the maximum recommended RPM in an emergency situation, such as passing, when required. A governor restricts the engine to a fixed maximum RPM, emergency need notwithstanding.

failures of truck and bus engines are commonly due to overheating and/or over-revving. All engines are rated at a certain horsepower at a particular RPM. However, this does not mean that it is safe to operate the engine at that RPM. Usually, to do so will cause early engine failure. Instead, consult the manufacturer's recommendations concerning the maximum permissible RPM for sustained operation. This usually coincides with the manufacturer's recommended governor setting. As an example, a particular engine is rated at 212 BHP at 3,000 RPM. However, the manufacturer adjusts the governor on this engine to 2,600 RPM at the factory. Therefore, 2,600 RPM should be the maximum speed the engine is operated at under continuous operation.

In the case where the recommended maximum operating RPM of the engine is not known, you may determine this yourself through some simple calculations. To do so, we may proceed as follows:

There is a generally-accepted rule-of-thumb concerning truck engines which limits the piston speed to 2100 feet per minute, or 2200 feet per minute providing an oil cooler is installed. Piston speeds in excess of this cause rapid stress and heat built-up, and engine damage may occur. Determine the stroke of the engine. This may be obtained by referring to the maintenance manual for the engine. Since the piston moves downwardly and upwardly during one complete revolution of the crankshaft, we must double the stroke to determine the piston travel per revolution.

Assuming an engine with a stroke of six inches, then 6 x 2 equals 12 inches piston travel per revolution. Then, dividing 2100 feet x 12 inches, (one foot) we obtain 2100 RPM.

It will be noted that the shorter the stroke, the higher the maximum permissible RPM. Typical maximum RPM versus stroke are:
For stroke lengths not shown here, the table may be

Stroke	Max. Recommended RPM
3"	4200
3 3/4"	3675
4 1/2"	3150
5 1/4"	2625
6"	2100

interpolated or extrapolated as required. When an engine oil cooler is installed, the maximum RPM may be increased approximately 100 RPM. The "maximum" refers to continuous or sustained operation, and not for brief spurts such as passing, etc.

We may go a step further and determine the corresponding road speed for the maximum RPM of the engine. To do so, we proceed as follows:

First, we must determine the rolling diameter of the rear wheel, and then calculate the circumference of the rolling diameter. The rolling diameter is twice the rolling radius, which should be measured from the center of the hub or axle to the rood surface. (This allows for tire deformation at the road surface).

Let us assume a rolling radius of 19.1 inches. (Rolling diameter then would be 19.1 x 2, or 38.2 inches) Multiplying 38.2 inches by 3.141 (pi) we obtain approximately 120 inches, or 10 feet. This means the vehicle moves 10 feet for each complete revolution of the rear wheel. Dividing 10 feet into 5,280 feet (1 mile) we obtain 528 revolutions per mile.

Next, we must determine the rear axle ratio of the bus. To do so, jack up one wheel of the bus. Mark a reference point on the drive shaft or universal joint. Turn the rear wheel two complete turns, while carefully counting the total number of revolutions made by the drive shaft or universal joint. This number of revolutions mode by the drive shaft or universal joint is equal to the rear axle ratio to 1.

(Six revolutions of the drive shaft during two revolutions of the rear wheel would equal a rear axle ratio of 6:1)

Assuming that the transmission is a 1:1 ratio in high gear, then the driveshaft RPM is equal to the engine RPM in high gear. For an overdrive transmission, the engine RPM will be less than the driveshaft RPM in overdrive. (Typically .81:1 in overdrive).

If the vehicle were traveling at the rate of one mile in one minute, (true 60 MPH), and the rear wheels rotated 528 times during that one minute and one mile, then the engine RPM would be 528 x rear axle ratio, (assuming a rear axle ratio of 6, then 528 x 6 equals 3168 RPM of the engine. Or, we may divide 3168 by 60, and obtain revolutions of the engine per mile per hour. (Approximately 53 engine RPM per mile per hour). If the engine has a 6" stroke, and is therefore limited to 2100 RPM, then the top speed equals 2100 divided by 53, or approximately 40 MPH.

A 4-½ inch stroke would equal 3150 divided by 53, or approximately 60 MPH, and so on.

Overdrive transmissions are desirable in a motor coach, as they permit lower engine RPM for the same road speed. Likewise, lower numerical ratios for the rear axle (for example, a rear axle ratio of 6:1 instead of 7:1, etc.) permit higher road speeds for the same engine RPM.

However, we may reach a point at which the coach has ample high speed, but lacks pulling power at low speeds. In this case, we must either compromise between road speed and pulling power, or, preferably, install an overdrive transmission for higher road speed, or install a two-speed rear axle, with a low range (high numerical ratio) for pulling, and a high range (low numerical ratio) for higher speed. Buses equipped with either an overdrive transmission or a two-speed rear axle are very much in demand for conversion into motor coaches, and usually command higher prices.

Many modern engines tend toward shorter strokes than the older engines, and therefore may operate at a higher RPM with less engine wear, Automobile engines are not designed to deliver their maximum torque for prolonged periods. Automotive-type engines should not be operated at more then about two-thirds of their maximum torque rating for long life expectancy.

Although not part of this chapter, rather than leave half of a page blank, I offer this additional photo.

This beautiful coach features a hardwood floor and a tile kitchen.

Like many top notch conversions I have seen, this unit uses individual dining chairs on castors. Other coaches employ standard recliners and other home-style furniture that is not anchored down.

While this maximizes comfort and convenience, these items need to be secured when on the road. An accident, sudden stop or even a sharp turn or steep incline would create havoc and would be unsafe.

Glossary of Terms

A.W.G.: American Wire Gauge.

Air Gap: The unobstructed vertical distance through the free atmosphere between the lowest opening from any pipe or faucet supplying water to a plumbing fixture and the floor-level rim of the fixture.

Anti-flooding Device: A primary safety control which causes the liquid fuel flow to be shut off upon a rise in fuel level or upon receiving excess fuel, and which operates before a hazardous discharge of fuel can occur.

Appliance Branch Piping: Any run of pipe or tubing, and fittings that is used to convey fuel from the main manifold to a fuel burning, heat-producing appliance or appliances.

Automatic Pilot Device: A device employed with gas burning equipment that will either automatically shut off the gas supply to the burner(s) being served or automatically actuate, electrically or otherwise, a gas shutoff device when the pilot flame is extinguished.

Battery Circuit: A circuit directly energized by a battery not in excess of 12 volts and does not include a low-energy circuit.

Branch Circuit Panel board: The necessary equipment, consisting of circuit breakers or switch and fuses arid their accessories, intended to constitute the main control and means of cutoff for the supply to the vehicle.

BTU: British Thermal Units. The quantity of heat required to raise the temperature of one pound of water one degree Fahrenheit.

Combination Compartment: A shower stall or recess that provides for a toilet and is of such size and proportions that it may not be occupied by more than one person at one time.

Common Vent: That part of a piping system that is designed and installed to vent more than one fixture.

Continuous Vent: A vertical vent that is a continuation of the drain to which it connects.

Critical Level: C-L or C/L marking on a backflow prevention device or vacuum breaker. A point established by a testing laboratory and stamped on the device by the manufacturer which determines the minimum elevation above the floor level rim of the fixture served on which the device may be installed.

Diameter: Unless stated otherwise, the nominal diameter as designated commercially.

Drain Coupler: The fitting designed and used ta connect the vehicle main drain outlet to the connector used for connecting the main drain outlet to the point of disposal.

Drain Outlet: The discharge end of the vehicle main drain to which the drain coupler is attached.

Drainage System: All the piping within or attached to the vehicle structure that conveys sewage or other liquid wastes to the drain coupler.

Dual System: An electrical system energized by a generator mounted on the vehicle and a supply assembly designed to be energized from on outside source of supply.

Duct: Conduits or passageways for conveying air to or from a heating appliance, but not including the plenum to which the duct is connected.

Flush Tank: That portion of a toilet that is designed to contain sufficient water to adequately flush the fixture.

Flush Valve: A flushing device located at the bottom of the flush tank.

Flushometer Valve: A device that discharges a predetermined quantity of water to a fixture for flushing purposes and is actuated by direct water pressure.

Gas Appliance Connector: A connector, used to convey fuel, three feet or less in length (six feet or less for gas ranges), between a gas outlet and a gas appliance in the same room with the outlet.

Gas Piping: All piping and tubing installed in or attached to a vehicle to convey fuel gas to fuel-burning, heat-producing appliances.

Gas Supply Connection: The terminal end of the gas piping system to which a gas supply connector is attached.

Gas Supply Connector: A detachable flexible connector designed to convey fuel gas from the gas supply to the vehicle gas supply connection.

Heat-producing Appliance: A heating or cooking appliance utilizing fuel or energy.

Horizontal: Any pipe or fitting which makes an angle of not more than 45 degrees from the horizontal.

Individual Vent: A pipe installed to vent a fixture

trap connected with the vent system above the fixture served and terminating outside the vehicle.

Input Rating: The maximum fuel-burning capacity of any warm-air furnace, recessed heater or burner expressed in British Thermal Units (BTU).

Longitudinal Center: The midpoint between the right and left side of the vehicle unit containing the utility connections.

Main Drain: The principal artery of the drainage system to which drainage branches may be connected.

Main Gas Piping Manifold: Gas piping which conveys gas from the gas supply connection to the first appliance branch piping.

Main Vent: The principal artery of the vent system to which vent branches may be connected.

Oil Piping System: All piping and tubing installed in or attached to a vehicle to convey fuel oil to fuel-burning, heat-producing appliances.

Plumbing Fixture: A fixture which is supplied with water or which receives liquid or liquid-borne wastes and which is directly or indirectly connected to the drainage system.

Power Supply Assembly: The cable, including the grounding conductors insulated from one another, the connectors, attachment plug cops, and all other fittings, grommets, or devices installed for the purpose of delivering energy from the source of electrical supply to the distribution panel within the vehicle.

Roof Jack: That portion of a heater flue or vent assembly, including the cap, insulating means, flashing, and ceiling plate, located in and above the roof of a vehicle.

Toilet Mechanical Seal: A toilet fitted with water-flushing device and mechanically sealed trap.

Toilet Recirculating Chemical: A self-contained, electrically-operated recirculating chemically-control led toilet.

Toilet Wet Flush: A toilet fitted with a water flushing device and integral trap.

Trap: A device designed and constructed to provide, when properly vented, a liquid seal that will prevent the back passage of air without materially affecting the flow of water-borne waste through it.

Trap Arm: That portion of the drainage system connecting a trap to its vent or wet-vented drain.

Trap Seal: The maximum vertical depth of liquid that a trap will retain, measured between the crown weir and the top of the dip of the trap.

Vent System: A pipe or pipes installed to provide a flow of air to or from a drainage system or to provide a circulation of air within such system to protect trap seals from siphonage and back pressure.

Vent Connector: Any pipe for conveying products of combustion from a fuel-burning appliance to a vent.

Vertical Pipe: A pipe which makes on angle of not more than 45 degrees with the vertical.

Waste Holding Tank: A liquid-tight tank for the temporary retention of water-borne waste.

Water Distribution System: All of the water piping within or attached to the vehicle, including the water supply connection.

Water Heater: An appliance for supplying hat water for other than space heating.

Water Supply Connection: The fitting or point of connection of the vehicle water distribution system designed for connection to a water supply.

Wet Vent: A vent that also serves as a drain.

Wet-Vented Drainage System: A specially designed system of drain piping which vents one or more plumbing fixtures by means of a common waste and vent pipe.

Table of Abbreviations

AC   Alternating Current (Usually 120 volts)
B.B.   Bunk Bed
B.C.   Base Cabinet
C.   Commode (or Broom Cabinet)
CAB   Cabinet
CH   Chest
DC   Direct Current (Usually 12 volts)
DWR   Drawer
DIN   Dinette
DIV   Divan
D.S.   Driver's Seat
F.B.   Full Bed
L   Lavatory
LPG   Liquefied petroleum Gas (Propane)
O.C.   Overhead Cabinet(s)
O/A   Standard drafting term for "Overall"
P.S.   Passenger Seat
R   Refrigerator
R.T.B. Reclining Twin Bed (or lounge)
SH   Shower
SK   Sink
ST   Stove (or Range/Oven)
STP.   Door Step
T   Toilet
T.B.   Twin Bed
V.   Vanity
W.   Wardrobe

Note: O.C. (overhead cabinets) are usually installed in all places where they do not interfere with bathrooms or wardrobes.

Omitted Sections

**The following chapters contained in the original editions of this book
are outdated and not included in the 2004 version.**

Chapter 20: Organizations of Interest to Motor Coach Owners

Chapter 21: Publications

Chapter 22: Obtaining Parts, Equipment, Accessories and Appliances

Chapter 23: The Buyer's Guide – obsolete

Appendix: (1971California Administrative Code) – obsolete

Numerous organizations, publications, new and used on-line appliance and
accessory stores are listed in our links page and are generally available.

http://www.rv-busconversions.com/buslinks.html

**If your state does not have an RV building code, refer to
NFPA 1192 Standard on Recreational Vehicles.
This book is available from the National Fire Protection Association
<u>http://www.nfpa.org</u>   Enter "1192" in the search box.**

Appendix

These are a few of the many bus conversion books available today. If your bookstore doesn't stock them, you can order them on-line at **http://www.rv-busconversions.com/** or write for a free bus conversion book catalog to:

Ben Rosander
PO Box 327
Marysville, WA 98270-0327

If you know of other bus conversion books or materials, please contact me. Thank you.

Select and Convert Your Bus…
by Ben Rosander

Bus Conversion Floor Plans
by Ben Rosander

Dreams on Wheels: Modern Do-it-Yourself Gypsies
by Ben Rosander

The Bus Converter's Bible
by Dave Galey

The Bus Garage Index
A "must have" when you are ready for the road.

The Bus Pages
A Yellow Pages style reference book for the bus industry

Beginner's Guide to Converted Coaches
by Larry Plachno

Classy Cabinets for Converted Coaches
by Dave Galey

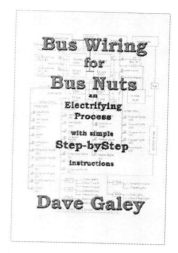

Bus Wiring for Bus Nuts
by Dave Galey

NFPA 1192: Standard on Recreational Vehicles

This book can be ordered from the
National Fire Protection Association
1 Batterymarch Park,
Quincy, Massachusetts 02169-7471
or on-line at: **http://www.nfpa.org**

Periodicals

These magazines are available at a substantial discount through
http://www.rv-busconversions.com/rvmagazines.html

Bus Conversions

Motorhome

Gypsy Journal

Acknowledgements

We wish to thank the following who contributed to this new edition.

Classic Manufacturing, Inc.
21900 U.S. 12
Sturgis, MI 49091
Toll Free: 1-800-826-1960
http://www.classicmfg.com/

Colonial Coach Lines
1600 James Drive
Mt. Prospect, Illinois 60056
http://www.colonialcoach.com/

ITT Industries - (FLOJET)
20 Icon
Foothill Ranch, CA 92610
1-800-2-FLOJET
http://www.flojet.com/

KUSTOM FIT HI-TECH Seating Products, Inc.
8990 Atlantic
South Gate, CA 90280
323-564-4481
http://www.kustomfit.com/

Staley Coach
933 - A West Old Hickory Boulevard
Madison, Tennessee 37115-3461
615-860-9485
http://www.staleycoach.com/

Walker Private Coach, Inc.
8281 RT 873
Slatington, PA 18080 (By appointment only)
610-767-8100
http://www.walkercoach.com/

Wayne Harper for "Michaela"

Chris Jeub for the Jeub Family Bus floor plan
http://www.jeubfamily.com/bus

Larry McGuire for the Scenicruiser

Joe Petty for "BruinGilda the AeroSwine"
http://www.pettypb.com/bus/index.htm

Rick and Myrna Russell

Chris and Lina Toughill for "Giddy-Up Go"

Index

Printed in the United States
221192BV00003B/8/A